Grandma,
I Need Your Prayers

Grandma,
I Need Your Prayers

Blessing Your Grandchildren through the Power of Prayer

Quin Sherrer * Ruthanne Garlock

ZONDERVAN™

GRAND RAPIDS, MICHIGAN 49530

ZONDERVAN™

Grandma, I Need Your Prayers
Copyright © 2002 by Quin Sherrer and Ruthanne Garlock

Requests for information should be addressed to:

Zondervan, *Grand Rapids, Michigan 49530*

Library of Congress Cataloging-in-Publication Data

Sherrer, Quin.
    Grandma, I need your prayers : blessing your grandchildren through the power of
prayer / Quin Sherrer and Ruthanne Garlock.
       p. cm.
    Includes bibliographical references.
    ISBN 0-310-24026-3
    1. Grandmothers—Prayer-books and devotions—English. 2. Grandchildren—
Religious life. I. Garlock, Ruthanne. II. Title.
    BV4847 .S48 2001
    248.3'2'0853–dc21   2001046640

Published in association with the literary agency of Ann Spangler & Associates, 1420 Pontiac Road SE, Grand Rapids, MI 49506.

Details and circumstances of certain events, and some names of persons and locations, have been changed to protect individuals' privacy.

Interior design by Nancy Wilson

Printed in the United States of America

02 03 04 05 06 07 08 09 /❖ DC/ 10 9 8 7 6 5 4 3

Dedicated to our grandchildren ...

Quin's:

Kara Nicole, Evangeline Noel, Ethan Keil
Lyden Benjamin, Victoria Jewett
Samuel Johannes

Ruthanne's:

Amanda Jean
Rachel Lynn, Lydia Marie, Joel David

I will make Your name to be remembered
in all generations;
therefore shall the people praise and give You
thanks forever and ever.

—Psalm 45:17 AMPLIFIED

Contents

Introduction   11

1. A Grandmother's Spiritual Influence   15

2. Praying for Spiritual Growth   33

3. Praying for Homes and Families   49

4. Praying for Friends and Schooling   65

5. Praying for Protection and Health   81

6. Praying for Hurting Grandchildren   97

7. Praying for Families Broken by Death or Divorce   115

8. Praying for Adopted Grandchildren and Stepgrandchildren   133

9. Praying for Prodigal Grandchildren   149

10. Praying for Choices and Turning Points   165

11. Taking the Role of Parent or Coparent   181

12. Leaving a Lasting Legacy   197

Epilogue   211
Appendix   214
Suggested Reading   219
Notes   221

Introduction

I got word of the birth of my first grandchild—Kara Nicole, born on the island of Kona, Hawaii—while I was speaking at a Christian retreat center in the mountains of Pennsylvania. When my prayer partner, Jane, went to get us early morning coffee, the hotel clerk told her that during the night a message had come that Kara had been born.

"You're a grandmother! A grandmother! A grandmother!" Jane shouted excitedly at me.

A grandmother. It was hard for me to comprehend the new title tacked to my name. A new identity. My three children were older when they married, and two of them had been married for several years. I had wondered at times whether I'd *ever* be a grandmother. No need to worry! Now, six years later, I have six grandchildren, one born during the writing of this book, giving Kara and her sister, Evie, a baby brother.

Three of my grandchildren were born overseas, so at first I could communicate with them only by letting them hear my voice on the phone. They responded with silence or cooing. But now all three families are just a short drive from us, and the grandkids call me "Mama Quin."

Our home quickly filled up with all the paraphernalia that goes with tending babies and toddlers—high chairs, baby beds, potty-chairs, swing set, T-ball stands, and a miniature basketball court. We also have children's books on prayer and character development, phonics games, puzzles, videos, and music tapes. I became a regular baby-sitter, since two of the grandchildren lived across the street for a couple of years.

My goal is to be the best grandmother I can be, to establish a Christian heritage my grandchildren won't forget. As I rock them, I sing and pray over them. When we stroll around the block, I tell them we're praying for our neighbors as we sing "Alleluia." We enjoy having parades with rhythm band instruments in our den while the vibrant old hymns play on the video. In the summer, I splash in the plastic pool with them, and in the winter, I cheer as they coast down our back-yard snowbank. Since most have entered preschool, I attend their performances and get acquainted with all their teachers.

If you were to drop by my house today, you'd probably find me sitting on the floor with two or three grandchildren building railroad stations out of plastic blocks, or drinking imaginary tea from tiny china cups, or sitting in a sandbox making sand castles. I'd be wearing my favorite sweatshirt that says, "Grandmas Are Antique Little Girls." I always stop whatever I'm doing to give them attention. When they stay overnight, we have the best times sharing and praying. Right now they are the most important people in my life whom I can influence for God's purposes.

I have a picture of all six of my grandchildren gathered around me on a stairway decorated with holiday holly. I carry it with me on out-of-town trips so I can see them smiling down at me from the bedside table. The wooden frame, a gift from a daughter, is carved with these words:

> Grandchildren bring sunshine into my heart
> And laughter into my household.
> Their visits may be long or short, but always memorable.
> I tell them my stories and they tell me theirs right back.
> It's my grandchildren that actually made me a grandparent,
> So I'm eternally grateful.
> They always bring such spirited joy into my life.
>
> —Author unknown

I don't remember having a grandmother who prayed for me. My maternal grandmother died just after I, the first granddaughter, was born at her home. My paternal grandmother was a pastor's wife, but I never was aware whether she prayed for her fourteen grandchildren. I remember that as a twelve-year-old, I sat on a stool at the feet of my blind great-grandmother, whose brothers had fought in the Civil War. Once, after telling me stories of that tragic war, she asked me to guide her hand to rest on the top of my head. Did she pray for me? I'd like to think so, but I will never know.

My mother, a wonderful long-distance grandmother to my three children, left me the only example I have to follow. She constantly kept in touch with them through phone calls, letters, or as many visits as she could manage, always letting each one know how special he or she was to her. Just as her prayers are affecting my children and grandchildren, I hope my prayers will affect the next generation.

Once, I saw a picture showing an elderly woman's lined hand with an open palm reaching out for a child's tiny hand, just inches away. The caption read, "If all the hands that reach could only touch." I envisioned a grandmother, reaching out to touch a grandchild, offering hope and love to her. A recent survey indicates that nearly 90 percent of grandparents do keep in touch with their grandchildren. We urge you not only to maintain contact with your grandchildren but also to pray for them.

If you are one of the more than sixty million Americans who have grandchildren, this book will motivate you to pray consistently and strategically for them, whether they live next door, across town, or halfway around the world. You will read stories which testify to the remarkable power of grandmothers' prayers. And in each chapter you will find Scriptures and prayers to help you pray regularly for each of your grandchildren.

May you be encouraged and challenged as you read of grandmas who share how they pray for the precious grandchildren God has given them. You will discover, as they have, that praying makes a difference in your grandchildren's lives.

—Quin Sherrer

A Grandmother's Spiritual Influence

I constantly remember you in my prayers. . . . I have been reminded of your sincere faith, which first lived in your grandmother Lois and in your mother Eunice and, I am persuaded, now lives in you also.

—2 Timothy 1:3, 5

When grandmothers are missing from a society, that society loses its link to the wisdom of the past and the traditions that make the tribe able to reflect on itself. . . . Being a grandmother is a constant learning and teaching experience, because as grandmothers, women must learn to apply yesterday's wisdom to today's challenges.

—Kristen Johnson Ingram,
I'll Ask My Grandmother—She's Very Wise

Mom, you're going to be a grandmother!"

When you first hear these words, the prospect of seeing a new generation raised up ignites hope, love, and purpose in your life. A grand opportunity awaits you to immediately begin praying for the spiritual, physical, and emotional well-being of your grandchild.

Perhaps you're wondering whether your prayers can actually make a difference in your grandchild's life. I (Quin) had an encounter one day that reminded me how much of a difference a grandmother's prayers can make.

"She Was Always Praying for Me"

"I'll bet you had a praying grandmother," I said to the professional basketball player I'd been chatting with while we were waiting in the Atlanta airport for our flight to be called.

"I did, but how did you know?" he asked, looking surprised.

"While we've been talking, you mentioned her several times and spoke about how much you love and admire her," I answered.

"Yes," he said softly, dropping his head. "When my mom left, my grandmother took me in to live with her. Through all those years, she prayed for me and encouraged me in every sport I ever tried. She always told me I could become a professional athlete if I set a goal, practiced for hours, and depended on God to strengthen me."

"And it looks like some of those prayers have been answered," I replied.

"She was always praying for me," he continued with a smile. "I could call her from anywhere I was playing a game, and she'd pray on the phone for me right then. She was a wonderful grandmother—old now but still praying."

What a tribute to a quiet little grandmother who poured her life and prayers into an abandoned grandson, never dreaming he would one day become a well-known athlete. And what an encouragement to praying grandmothers that their efforts are not in vain!

When the apostle Paul wrote to his spiritual son, Timothy (in the verse quoted at the beginning of this chapter), he acknowledged—for all generations to follow—the powerful influence of a godly grandmother. In this book, we hope to expand your vision to see just how far-reaching your spiritual influence upon your grandchildren can be. Keeping a heart connection with them is the important thing, whether they live close to you or many miles distant. We'll share creative ideas through stories of other grandmothers to show you how. Also, we'll provide guidelines to help you establish a scriptural strategy for praying for your grandchildren.

Impacting the Next Generation

Most grandmothers probably have given their best years to rearing their children. They've sacrificed, worried, scolded, and encouraged—and through it all prayed that God would keep their children safe and help them become mature adults. As author Barbara Johnson says, "We're always hoping that something we instilled in them *might* show up, even when we've started to think it's too late."[1]

Some, feeling their work is now over, may sigh with relief when their children leave home and later start families of their own. Others may be tempted to spend their best energy pursuing a relaxing lifestyle filled with travel and hobbies. A few may feel a bit depressed, wondering why they seem to have no purpose now that their children are out of the nest. Whatever our situation, God still has more kingdom work for us moms to do, especially when it comes to our grandchildren.

Even if you don't yet have any, it's never too early to begin praying for your grandchildren. Whether a child is in the womb or is only a dream, you can influence your future grandchildren for good through your prayers. They are our link to the future, and our faithfulness to pray for them can greatly impact this new generation.

With the pressure on families today, grandchildren need our hugs, reassurance, and wisdom more than ever. And most of all, they need our prayers and godly influence. Grandmothers usually are fond of giving gifts to their grandchildren, but the greatest and most lasting gift they can give is one of faithful prayer. Many children have no one except a grandma to pray for them.

"What Grandma Meant to Me"

When we asked people to share what a grandmother's spiritual influence has meant in their lives, we got a variety of answers.

- "My grandmother gave me a sense of security and stability and taught me many practical things. Because my mom was a teenager when I was born, she was too young and immature to add that dimension to my life."

- "Granny was my hero; she always remembered my birthday and other special moments in my life. But most of all, she prayed for me."

- "My grandmother read my favorite stories to me over and over; then I'd let her read me her favorite ones from her well-worn Bible."

- "Grandma Jessie had twelve children and helped manage a farm for much of her life, yet she always seemed calm and serene. I never saw her get upset or raise her voice. She left me with an enduring sense that whatever comes, faith in God remains imperturbable. Nothing ever wins against it."

- "My great-grandmother's prayers have followed me from the day I was born. Like a heavenly searchlight, her prayers have exposed darkness in my life."

- "I remember Friday nights at Mammaw's home and her tucking me into a feather bed as she prayed over me. Then came Saturday morning in her busy kitchen, when she made and sold tuna sandwiches and homemade pies to have extra money for an offering to the church. She was my first prayer partner, and remembering the intimacy she had with the Lord has given me the security to know he is there for me when I call."

- "Grandma Bea treats me like the age I am and doesn't talk down to me."

- "My grandmother didn't live nearby, but she wrote me many letters. Every one of them ended with, 'Stay close to the Lord; he's coming soon.' I was—and still am—enamored with heaven because of her letters."

- "Grandma MuMu could not communicate well in English, but I loved hearing her sing her beloved Finnish hymns and watching her read her large Bible at the dining table. I saw her life as a book; I read from her and learned the value of her beautiful character, compassion, and godliness."

- "I never knew my grandmothers, but God has placed women in my life who have shown me the power of a praying grandmother and who have been examples to me."

- "I can still 'see' every nook and cranny of Grandma John's house. I knew I could always go there—a safe place where I was totally accepted. She played the piano and sang hymns when I visited her, giving me a love for hymns that I still have today and have tried to pass on to my own children and grandchildren. Wholeness and a love for life are what she taught me; she had an awe and reverence for God and all his creation that she passed on to me."

I (Ruthanne) usually saw my Grandma McBee only at reunions of my mom's family, except for one summer when I stayed with her and Grandpa for two weeks. My strongest memory of her is how she loved to read her Bible and prepare lessons for the Sunday school class of boys she taught. When I think of her, I picture a stooped little woman in a faded apron and cotton dress, sitting in a rocking chair reading by dim lamplight. In later years, I was amazed to learn that famous baseball player Mickey Mantle had often visited her Sunday school class with a boyhood friend.

My husband, John, had a very different experience with his maternal grandmother, who was the daughter of Irish immigrants. He shares his story.

"Her Anchor Was Prayer"

"My first clear memories of Grandmom Trotter, as we called my mother's mom, are of her visit with us in Colorado Springs, where my father was a pastor. I was five years old. 'How old are you, Grandmom?' I asked her one day. After extracting a promise that I wouldn't tell anyone, she told me she was sixty-six, an age which seemed to me ancient at the time. When I was eleven years old, I got to know my grandmother better than most people ever have the chance to experience.

"My younger sister, Ruth, and I had been sent back to the United States from West Africa for health reasons. We lived with Grandmom in a small, shabby frame house in New Jersey while my parents were finishing the last year of their four-year term as missionaries in the northern territories of Ghana.

"During that year I became really aware of Grandmom's deep faith, her love of the Bible, and her discipline of prayer. She faithfully maintained daily 'family devotions' for the three of us and often spoke earnestly of spiritual things. I learned from her that prayer is central, not auxiliary, for a Christian. Also, my first experience of telling others about Jesus came that year as I led several neighbor children to accept him as Lord.

"Grandmom was used to austerity and knew how to make do with very little. We grew potatoes, tomatoes, carrots, and cabbage next to our little house, which was heated by a coal furnace in the basement. A block of ice in an icebox kept our milk cool. Cooking was done on a coal stove. Grandmom was sober, sometimes

Essential Prayer Keys

Years ago while attending a writer's conference, I (Quin) sat across the dinner table from Catherine Marshall, whom I had long admired. Knowing her reputation as an author and also as a praying mother, I asked her, "Can you give me some advice on how to pray more effectively for my three children?"

"Be as specific in your prayers as you can, and plant waiting prayers for your children's future," she advised. Then she asked, "When you pray, do you really expect anything to happen?"

I pondered that question. Do I really expect anything to happen when I pray? I can tell you now that without a doubt, I do!

I not only listened to her advice, but I went home to dig through the Bible to read everything I could find on prayer as I endeavored to pray for my children—and see results. Now many years later, I use these same biblical principles in praying for my grandchildren. Though I share here some things I do in my private prayer times, I'm sure you can add to this list.

Be specific. I pray practical but specific prayers for my grand-children. I base this on a parable Jesus told about a man who wakes up his friend at midnight to ask for exactly three loaves of bread for his unexpected company (see Luke 11:5).

Be persistent. The man in the parable knocks continuously until his friend gets out of bed to answer his request. This isn't say-ing that prayers are needed to overcome God's reluctance to answer. Rather, this parable encourages us to be bold and per-sistent when we pray. Jesus said to ask, seek, knock—a con-tinuous asking, seeking, knocking (see Luke 11:8–10). I find myself in persistent prayer until I see a resolution to my grandchild's situation.

Be in agreement. I usually ask a prayer partner (my husband, a close friend, or a prayer support team) to pray in agreement with me concerning a pressing need. Jesus gives us the basis for prayers of agreement (see Matt. 18:19–20). For seventeen years I prayed with another mother on the phone for five minutes a day, five days a week. We were just two mothers concerned about our children's welfare, both spiritual and physical. Because that was such a positive experience, when I became a grandmother I began praying with grandmother friends. We pray for each other's grandchildren regularly, again by phone. Sometimes I contact them by e-mail when there is a crisis such as a grandchild in the hospital.

Be Bible based. As we get better acquainted with the Bible, we grow to know God better and to understand how to pray in accordance with his will. We learn what he says about salva-tion, health, family values, the abundant life on earth, and heaven's promises. I often find a Bible verse I can turn into a prayer for the need of a grandchild. The Psalms are a good place to start with Scripture prayers.

Be open to the Holy Spirit. After ascending to heaven, Jesus sent the Holy Spirit to help us pray what is on God's heart. Whatever our grandchildren's circumstances or crises, we invite the Holy Spirit to show us how to pray. Sometimes we may find ourselves praying things we could never have "thought up" on our own (see Rom. 8:26–27).

Be submitted to God's plan. We should never presume God is going to answer according to our preconceived ideas or in our desired timeframe. Presumption means assuming God will answer me in the way I envision and in my timetable. Faith, on the other hand, is a supernatural ability to trust God when he has spoken to my heart, trusting him to fulfill his will in his time and in his way. Often this "inner trust" or faith level comes after time spent in prayer, listening and waiting on him.

Be thankful. Present prayer requests to God with thanksgiving, thanking him in advance for answering your prayer his way (see Phil. 4:6).

Be willing to fast. Those serious enough to abstain from food have found fasting and prayer often yield one or more of these results: direction and answers from God, a deeper understanding of Scripture, a closer walk with God, a humbling of oneself, a healing, or even a deliverance. If you have a physical problem or are on medications, be careful about the type of fast you undertake. There are other things besides food we can give up to concentrate on a prayer project.

Trust him always. When it seems that our grandchildren are in a hopeless situation, we can admit that "we have no power ... [nor do we] know what to do, but our eyes are upon you" (2 Chron. 20:12). We don't know how or when our answer to prayer is coming, but we praise him for his loving-kindness and mercy. It's always too soon to quit praying.*

---

*Adapted from Quin Sherrer, *Miracles Happen When You Pray* (Grand Rapids: Zondervan, 1997), 16–19.

grim, but never mean. I don't remember any laugh more boister-
ous than a hearty chuckle. Our care was her mission, and she was
diligent about it. I had several bouts with malaria that year, and
she was my nurse.

"What with all the household work of cooking, cleaning, gardening, washing and patching clothes, and darning socks, she had
little time to spare. Firing the furnace and picking off the potato
bugs in the garden was my job when I was well enough. But what
time she had to herself she always spent reading the Bible and
praying. How diligent she was to intercede for Ruthie and me, and
for my parents, who were so far away! And when she prayed, you
somehow knew God was listening.

"When Grandmom Trotter passed away in her nineties, I was
a missionary in Africa and had not seen her for years. As an adult
I'd never had the opportunity to spend time with her. But I look
back and realize what a rock of stability she was for me in that
boyhood time of ill health, poverty, and insecurity. She was an
anchor of my life, and her anchor was prayer."

Special Weekends

Grandmother Mary, who lives in Alaska, spends one special
weekend each year alone with her granddaughter, Nicole. She
began this tradition when Nicole turned five. Her own grandmother was full-blooded Haida Indian and had spent time teaching her when she was small. Mary feels spending a special weekend
with Nicole is a way she can share that legacy with her only granddaughter.

After Mary and Nicole check into a hotel, they go shopping,
swimming, and finally dress up for dinner in a restaurant. Then
they return to their hotel for the best time of all, talking for hours
before going to sleep. They pray for many diverse things, ranging
from Nicole's school projects to her future husband.

The weekend is always a surprise to Nicole; Mary schedules it
with Nicole's mom, who knows her daughter's activity calendar.
When Nicole was small, they would take along Indian dolls to play

with. Mary would use a gray-haired "grandma" doll to talk to the little girl doll about manners, character building, biblical principles, and decisions Nicole will one day face. But now the dolls have been put aside, and Mary and fifteen-year-old Nicole talk woman to woman.

"As I pray aloud for her, I ask God to reveal his plan for her life, just as my Christian grandmother did for me when I was young," Mary said. "Once, when Nicole was nine, I took her with me to a Christian retreat where I was speaking, and there she had a deep spiritual experience with the Lord."

Mary always looks forward to this time, as it gives her the opportunity to pour spiritual truths and blessings into Nicole's young life. Also, the hands-on instruction helps nurture the talents and gifts God has placed in her granddaughter. When the storms of life occur, Mary knows Nicole will be aware that the Lord's arms are around her and will sustain her, even as her grandmother's arms have been around her, guiding her all these years.

The two do spend other times together, but they still set aside this one special weekend each year. Mary says she's watched her granddaughter's character unfold so beautifully as she has shared with her by phone or in person about God's purposes for her life.

Bestowing Blessings

Dr. Mary Ruth Swope, an author and nutritionist, was influenced by the godly life of her grandmother. When Mary Ruth was only six months old, Grandmother Lutz came to live with the family. From the start, she prayed over her infant granddaughter. As Mary Ruth grew, Grandmother Lutz not only prayed aloud with her, but she also played games with her, read her stories, and helped her memorize poetry. The two enjoyed many happy hours together as Grandmother Lutz taught Mary Ruth to sew, knit, crochet, tat, and quilt. Later Mary Ruth realized her grandmother had become her ideal role model.

As Mary Ruth thought about the tremendous impact her grandmother had had on her life, she longed to impress her seven-year-old grandson, Daniel, in a similar way. However, the many miles separating them made it impossible for her to be with him regularly.

Then she had an idea. Why couldn't she bless her grandson every time she spoke to him on the telephone? That would be a way to convey her personal and spiritual values to Daniel when she couldn't be with him.

That's exactly what she did. The first two times she spoke Scripture verses as blessings over him on the telephone, Daniel replied, "Thank you, Grandmother." But the next time she called, after they'd talked a while, he asked, "Aren't you going to bless me today?" Her heart jumped as she realized God was confirming to her how meaningful the blessings had been to Daniel, so she continued the tradition weekly.

Each time she prayed with Daniel on the phone, Mary Ruth would focus on a different area—praying blessings for his physical health, his spiritual and emotional needs, his educational interests, and his relationships with friends and family members. Doing this regularly made her feel much closer to her grandson.[2]

Today Daniel is an accomplished violinist who also composes music, and he is still grateful for his grandmother's prayers and blessings, which he receives regularly.

For sons and daughters in biblical times, receiving a blessing from the patriarch of the family was a momentous event. For instance, Jacob not only imparted a blessing to each of his twelve sons; he also spoke blessings to two of his grandsons (see Gen. 48:15–16, 20). And Jesus gathered children in his arms, put his hands on them, and blessed them (see Mark 10:13–16).

In their book *The Blessing*, authors Gary Smalley and John Trent further explain this principle.

A family blessing includes:
- Meaningful touch
- A spoken message
- Attaching "high value" to the one being blessed
- Picturing a special future for the one being blessed
- An active commitment to fulfill the blessing

When God blessed us with the gift of His Son, it was His *Word* that "became flesh and dwelt among us" (John 1:14). God has always been a God of the spoken word.

While the blessing is an ancient practice, it still holds important keys to granting genuine acceptance. From a blessing to the firstborn, to special words of love and acceptance for each child, the blessing remains a part of Jewish family life today. For the Christian parents [and grandparents] who have the hope and reality of Jesus, the Messiah, and His love, their blessing can be even more powerful.[3]

Beth, the mother of teenagers Anna and Abram, was blessed to have had godly grandparents while she was growing up. Grandma Louise and Grandpa Don were now in their nineties, and before the Lord took them home, she wanted them to touch the lives of her children. So she and the kids traveled from Colorado to California to visit the children's great-grandparents and ask them to lay hands on Anna and Abram to speak blessings over them.

"I'm grateful we made the trip before Grandma Louise died," Beth said. "Grandpa Don, now ninety-four, lives in a home for seniors, but each morning, he wakes up excited about what God might do that day. He conducts a regular Bible class for younger folk who come to learn from his wisdom. Recently, my husband went to visit Grandpa just to kneel at his feet and ask him to lay hands on him and impart blessings into his life. It's a wonderful legacy that we have."

Blessing and Prayer of Commitment

When Dee learned that her daughter, Dena, was expecting, she was excited about becoming a grandmother for the first time. Granddad Dick Eastman, president of Every Home for Christ and author of several outstanding books on prayer, believed he was to fast the entire month of October, the month Dena was expected to give birth to their first grandchild.

When Dee accompanied her daughter for a routine prenatal exam a week before the due date, doctors noted the baby was in a breech position. They needed to perform a cesarean section within hours. Granddad-to-be Dick, who was on the eighth day of his fast, was out of town, but Dee called immediately to alert him to pray.

As doctors prepared Dena for surgery, the monitor showed the baby's heart rate was falling. Concerned for the baby's health, Dee and her son-in-law, John, and Dena's parents gathered around Dena's bed to pray. They prayed for the baby's heart to function properly, for him to live and not die, and for all those involved in the birthing process to have God's wisdom. Then while John stayed with Dena, the others continued praying in the waiting room.

After some anxious moments, John, cradling his newborn son in his arms, walked into the waiting room to introduce little Jack to his grandmother Dee and his great-grandparents. "He was whole and healthy and beautiful, for which we praised God," said Dee.

Dick continued fasting through that month, praying for baby Jack. On the last day of the month, Granddad Dick and Grandmother Dee gathered for a special prayer and blessing service for the baby with little Jack's parents in the home of the other set of grandparents.

As a guide for their prayer, they chose the book *Living and Praying in Jesus' Name*, which Dick had coauthored. Baby Jack's parents and grandparents went down the list of thirty-one scriptural names for Jesus, praying that these attributes of Christ's nature and character would be developed in his life. Blessings were spoken over him with the words of promise associated with each title. Dick concluded by praying a prayer of commitment over his grandson.

Grandmother Dee held the baby most of the time as prayers and blessings were spoken over him. Amazingly, little Jack, without so much as a whimper, kept his eyes open, looking up at each one of them for the entire two hours of prayer. They videotaped the event so that when he gets older, Jack can watch the prayer service and know this is part of his spiritual heritage.

"Since I feel I'm to do this for each grandchild in the future, I jokingly asked both my daughters if they would please limit the size of their families," Dick said, laughing. "I was quite hungry by the end of that month!"

Here are a few of the thirty-one Scripture names of Jesus that the family prayed for Jack.

- A Wall of Fire (protection): Zechariah 2:5
- A Sure Foundation (stability): Isaiah 28:16
- The Way, the Truth, and the Life (purpose): John 14:6
- The Lord of Peace (comfort): 2 Thessalonians 3:16
- The Hidden Manna (provision): Revelation 2:17
- My Rock (refuge): Psalm 31:3[4]

A Lasting Memory

When I (Ruthanne) married my husband, John, he was a widower, a single parent who leaned heavily upon the family of his late wife for the emotional support they could give his two daughters. That family accepted me with open hearts, and I soon realized that my stepdaughters' Grandma Rains was a strong spiritual influence in the lives of *all* her grandchildren, not just the two in our house. One of them, Jill, shares her memories of this exceptional matriarch who lived to age 102.

"When I was small, I often spent the night at Grandma Rains' house. At bedtime we would kneel beside the bed to pray. First she would give thanks for our health, for our home, and for our many blessings. Then she began praying for her six children's families one by one, starting with the oldest and mentioning by name each family member.

"When she got to her fifth child—who had passed away before I ever knew her—she prayed for Uncle John, now married to Aunt Ruthanne, and for their children. Extra time was spent on them because they were full-time missionaries living overseas, and to Grandma they were saints. By the time she had called by name every child and his or her spouse, and every grandchild and great-grandchild, I was almost asleep. I thought she would *never* finish! I listened to her prayers for years and always paid attention to see whether she would accidentally skip somebody, but she never did.

"I grew older and married. During a time when my marriage

was in trouble, I asked Grandma to pray for me. I could go to sleep at night knowing that she was on her knees in prayer. What a wonderful comfort I had, knowing that no matter how big our family grew, I always had a praying grandma. Every child should be so blessed!"

Planting Seeds

The Bible instructs us to "not forget the things your eyes have seen or let them slip from your heart as long as you live. Teach them to your children and to their children after them" (Deut. 4:9). I (Quin) try to speak godly principles into the lives of our grandchildren whenever possible.

Often I will say to one of them, "God has a purpose for your life, and I'm praying God will prepare you for that purpose." While they may be too young to understand the implications of my words, I am planting seeds for their future understanding. In fact, I have hung this Scripture plaque on my kitchen wall: "The LORD will fulfill his purpose for me" (Ps. 138:8). I personalize and repeat it over and over to each grandchild, "The Lord will fulfill his purpose for you, Samuel."

We can encourage our grandchildren to develop their God-given abilities by praying for them and teaching them to talk to God even when they are toddlers. I've written our family's history to pass on to my grandchildren to help them understand their spiritual heritage. I'm also keeping a separate journal noting the little things I hear them say or watch them do that indicate their understanding of the gospel message. I pray this tradition will extend even to their children.

Like many grandparents, we keep a collection of Christian children's books, videos, and music tapes at our house. We read, read, read to our grandkids! The story of the walls of Jericho falling down is as exciting to our grandsons as it might have been for the Hebrew children watching that event thousands of years ago. They reenact the scene over and over in our den, playing toy trumpets and watching their large wall of blocks fall down.

Praying for a Spiritual Harvest

One grandmother wrote of how she loved baby-sitting two of her grandchildren after their elementary school was out and before their mother got home from work.

"I've always believed that we grandparents can impart deeper spiritual truths to our grandchildren than our children can, as they are twenty-something years younger," she said. "Sometimes I sense that I am viewing the happenings in those youngster's lives from a different perspective than the one their parents have. God helps me see the circumstances from his point of view, then he shows me how to pray with discernment."

It's true. Grandparents with a strong foundation of faith demonstrate by their lifestyle how to withstand the storms of life. Often a grandmother's involvement in the lives of grandchildren who are experiencing instability at home is crucial to their survival. But perhaps the most important role for a grandparent is simply to pray faithfully for those children, knowing that the seeds of prayer we plant today will yield a harvest of blessing in the future.

Our commitment to pray for our grandchildren and bestow blessings upon them whenever we can will impact their lives in countless positive ways. But more than that, our actions toward this generation will influence many generations to follow. We can't afford to miss this awesome opportunity God has given us.

Prayer

Lord, thank you for the spiritual and practical influence I have in my grandchildren's lives. Even if I don't see them often, I pray the time we do spend together—whether in person or on the phone—will be quality time. Show me ways to bless them, encourage them, and be available for them. Please reveal to me when and how to pray for their spiritual, physical, and emotional well-being. I want to be a godly grandmother they can emulate; thank you for equipping me to do this. Amen.

Helpful Scriptures

May the words of my mouth and the meditation of my heart
be pleasing in your sight,
O LORD, my Rock and my Redeemer.

—Psalm 19:14

One generation will commend your works to another;
they will tell of your mighty acts.
They will speak of the glorious splendor of your majesty. . . .
They will tell of the power of your awesome works,
and I will proclaim your great deeds.

—Psalm 145:4–6

Know therefore that the LORD your God is God; he is the
faithful God, keeping his covenant of love to a thousand generations of those who love him and keep his commands.

—Deuteronomy 7:9

Scripture Prayer

Lord, I pray for my grandchildren [names], holding unswervingly to the hope we profess, for he who promises is faithful [Heb. 10:23].

Thank you for your faithfulness!

Related Scripture References

Deuteronomy 11:18–21; 30:19–20
Proverbs 31:25–27

Praying for Spiritual Growth

I pray that out of his glorious riches he may strengthen you with power through his Spirit in your inner being, so that Christ may dwell in your hearts through faith. And I pray that you, being rooted and established in love, may ... know this love that surpasses knowledge—that you may be filled to the measure of all the fullness of God.

—Ephesians 3:16–19

With technological advances decreasing our emotional capacity to cope, children can be a royal nuisance. They want our attention at the most inopportune times. They are loud when we crave quiet. They ask a steady stream of questions. . . . Children are not convenient. Yet they are exquisite unopened gifts, simply waiting for a word to open them like flowers before the sun.

—Fawn Parish, *Honor: What Love Looks Like*

As grandparents, we are in a unique position to help steer our grandchildren in the ways of the Lord and encourage them in their spiritual growth. How we yearn for them to have Christ dwell in their hearts even at an early age.

If a child's relationship with God becomes well grounded while he or she is very young, the stormy adolescent years are less likely to weaken that foundation. We can strengthen the foundation by fostering a healthy self-image and by showing appreciation when our grandchildren exhibit godly traits or make wise choices. As they grow older, we can let them know we're praying that they will fulfill the purpose God has planned for them.

In this chapter you will learn from other grandmothers' experiences how you can influence your grandchildren by example and also how you can pray effectively for their spiritual development.

Blessing Them from the Moment of Birth

Carol felt honored when she was invited into the delivery room for the births of four of her grandchildren. Two were C-sections, and there was some degree of intensity in the room as she stood praying for peace and the safe delivery of her next grandchild.

"In the case of the C-sections, I stood behind the mother and prayed silently as the surgical team assembled," Carol said. "Then I continued praying during the administration of the anesthesia and through the delivery. When the baby arrived, I spoke a quiet prayer of thanksgiving and blessing over the newborn, calling out the baby's name and affirming its welcome to earth and to our family."

Arlene told us that she asked God to allow her to be present for the birth of each of her grandchildren and that even her daughters-in-law had said they wanted her to be with them in the delivery room.

"I asked the Lord to let me know when it was time for me to buy an airline ticket, which was necessary in some cases," she said. "God allowed me to arrive in time for the births of all eight grandchildren. Each time I entered the delivery room, I would thank him for being Lord over our families, over the babies' lives, and over everything that would happen in that room. I declared the blood covenant of the Lamb of God over each birth and prayed against any works of the enemy on behalf of each child. I asked God to release his love and peace to all those in the delivery room and to help the doctors to be 'skilled artisans' as they did their work."

Arlene refers to one grandson, who was born prematurely, as their miracle baby. "We claimed his numbered days, according to Psalm 139:16," she said. "I felt confident he would live, because God had quickened this verse to me: 'The LORD God formed the man from the dust of the ground and breathed into his nostrils the breath of life, and the man became a living being' (Gen. 2:7). We are so grateful that today this child is nine years old and very healthy."

Many of our grandmother friends make such efforts to be present for the birth of a grandchild, especially since hospital policy now generally allows family members in birthing rooms. They feel this is one way to pass on a spiritual blessing.

As the children grow, you can talk to them about God at a level they can understand, maybe when you are tucking a small one into bed or shooting hoops with an older child at the park. You can let them know the Bible is the most important book in the universe and that it has the answers to all their questions. Also share with them the value of prayer, citing examples of how God has answered prayers in your family.

Grandparents can contribute to their grandchildren's spiritual growth by giving them books, videos, games, and puzzles based on biblical principles; there are hundreds to choose from for every age. Several times a year, I (Quin) take my grandchildren to the Christian bookstore and let them select books or videos within a certain price range as a merit award for something they've done. At other times, I buy ones I know they like, then hide them away until they visit me.

It seems we have our most spiritual talks when they sleep over at my house and beg for a good-night story. I usually select one in advance on topics such as angels, feeding the poor, being a Good Samaritan, or obeying their parents. After reading the story, I ask them questions and we discuss the topic.

We grandparents can gain ideas, comfort, and prayer support from other Christians—and reap great rewards when we see results in our grandchildren's spiritual growth.

Interceding for Their Salvation

To pray for our grandchildren means to intercede for them. That is, we stand between them and God, asking him to intervene in situations in their lives. Many praying grandmothers call this "standing in the prayer gap" for their grandchildren.

If your grandchildren don't yet know the Lord, you can pray with assurance that it is his will for them to accept him. Jesus' whole purpose in coming to earth was to "seek and to save that which was lost." He doesn't want anyone to perish but desires that everyone comes to repentance.[1] To lead your grandchildren in prayer to receive Jesus, you may want to have them pray something similar to this:

Jesus, I believe you are God's Son, who came to earth, died on the cross for my sins, and rose from the dead. Please forgive me for the wrong things I have done, as I choose to forgive those who have hurt me. I accept you as my Lord and Savior and ask you to be my best friend. Help me to live in a way that pleases you. Thank you that I will one day be with you in heaven. Amen.

Suggestions for Prayer

Once our grandchildren have a personal relationship with Jesus, we can:

Pray they will develop the fruit of the Holy Spirit in their lives: "love, joy, peace, patience, kindness, goodness, faithfulness, gentleness and self control" (Gal. 5:22–23).

Pray they will truly comprehend how much God loves them instead of thinking the Christian faith is a list of do's and don'ts.

Pray they will listen for the Holy Spirit, obeying God's voice.

Pray for their parents to have wisdom and patience as they teach and guide the character development of their children.

Developing Godly Character

One day five-year-old Lyden was visiting me (Quin) when his four-year-old cousin did something to upset him. "Excuse me, Mama Quin," he said, "I have to get off alone and give Jesus this anger." A little later he came back smiling. "That's what Mom said I have to do when I get so mad I can't stand it. I have to give away my anger, and Jesus gives me his peace in its place," he explained.

A few days later, he was visiting my house and again showed anger. "Lyden, don't you need to give that anger to Jesus and ask him to forgive you?" I asked him. I always want to reinforce his mother's rules and encourage him to honor his parents.

As we pray, we can paraphrase Ephesians 4:2–3 in this way: "Lord, I pray that my grandchildren will be humble and gentle, that they'll be patient, bearing with one another in love. May they make every effort to keep the unity of the Spirit through the bond of peace, as your Word tells us to do."

Learning at Grandmother's Knee

Our friend JoAnne can remember when she was five years old, sitting on a stool at her grandmother's knee learning the Lord's Prayer, and having the Bible read to her over and over. It was her grandmother who taught her to memorize the Psalms and helped her learn the old hymns of the church.

"When she tucked me in bed at night, Granny Ida would thank God for the day in a long prayer," JoAnne said. "In the morning, she'd wake me and ask me to join my 'amen' to her prayer in praising him for a new day. She would say, 'Good morning, God! This is your day and I will find reasons to praise you all day.' Whatever came up during the day, she'd stop and talk to the Lord about it, carrying on a conversation with him as though he was right there in the room. She persuaded me he was; she made God as real as the man next door. Whenever I could, I'd go down to her house to spend the night because she loved me so unconditionally."

Granny Ida encouraged JoAnne to talk to Jesus as her best friend, assuring her that he would help her grow up to be a godly woman. To this day, JoAnne prays like her grandmother did, talking to God in a conversational tone and offering much thanksgiving and praise.

"Now I'm a gray-haired grandma myself, and I pray each day for my own grandchildren," JoAnne said. "I get to see them only once every other year, but I know my prayers have an impact. And I can pass a godly legacy to them through phone conversations. I'm mentoring a couple of young mothers and teaching them how to pray for their children. Sometimes I feel that I've adopted their kids as my own grandchildren."

Some grandmas, unlike JoAnne, have the blessing of being able to see their grandchildren more often. In the following story, Sandy shares an unexpected hands-on mentoring opportunity she had with her granddaughter. Because such opportunities often come without warning, we need to be alert and ready to make the most of them.

Being a "Good Grandma"

For several years, Sandy's grandchildren lived so far away that they seldom saw one another. It was a happy day when her son-in-law got a job transfer and the family moved close enough for more frequent visits. Sandy would volunteer to baby-sit in order to spend time with the children.

One day her ten-year-old granddaughter, Julie, asked for her help with a school assignment. "We've been studying about different emotions in our class," she said. "The teacher asked each student to pick one of them and give a report to the class about it. But I want to use Scripture verses with mine. Grandma, can you help me?"

Sandy was delighted to search the Bible with the fifth-grader, exploring the many possibilities from which to choose. Finally Julie made her decision.

"A lot of kids in my class don't have peace and joy," she said. "If I share some of these Scriptures, then they will know that God can give it to them." She chose two or three verses from the many that Grandma Sandy had helped her find.

A few days later Sandy called her granddaughter to see how the class had received her talk. "Some of the kids laughed at me when I talked about God," Julie reported. "But that's okay because I have peace and joy and the ones who laughed don't. But now they know where they can get it!"

Sandy is pleased that Julie has such a great desire for her friends to know the Lord. She decided early on that in addition to praying for her grandchildren, she wanted to be involved in their lives so she could have a positive spiritual influence on them.

"One reason I feel strongly about this is because my experience with my own grandmother was so negative," she said. "Grandma lived with us part of the time when I was growing up, but she nearly always was grouchy and intolerant. If I displeased her, she would hit me with her cane. Once, she threw cold water on me and my friend when she was annoyed because we came skipping through the house. I decided I was going to be a 'good grandma' and have a loving relationship with my grandkids. We enjoy playing games together, and they always feel free to talk to me about anything that's bothering them. And that gives me better insight on how to pray for them."

One grandmother says she prays for her grandsons from Psalm 112 and for her grandaughters from Proverbs 31. She also prays these four things for all of them:

1. That no weapon formed against them will prosper.
2. That they will have divine appointments for their future mates.
3. That she will always be an encourager to them.
4. That they will be able to stand before Jesus one day and say, "I have glorified you on earth; I have finished the work you gave me to do."

The Likeness of Jesus

Grandmother Joyce has three grandchildren who live in the South Pacific, where their dad is a missionary dentist. She sees them maybe once every year or two. When her first grandchild was born, she prayed he would grow up in the likeness of Jesus, based on Luke 2:52: "And Jesus grew in wisdom and stature, and in favor with God and men."

"I felt this verse revealed a wealth of desirable traits to pray for my precious new grandchild," she said, "so I wrote his name on that page of my Bible and began praying it daily for him."

Today David is almost eleven and there are other grandchildren now—Olivia, Hanna, and Katie. Through the years this has been Grandma Joyce's most consistent prayer for all of them, with God showing her how to apply it to specific circumstances and needs in their lives.

"Lord, I'm thankful David is doing so well in school," she would pray. "But as he grows, may he learn more and more to treasure 'the riches of the wisdom and knowledge of God'" (Rom. 11:33).

Here are other examples of how she prays Luke 2:52:

"Father, as my grandchildren move so far away, give them the ability to make good new friends; may they increase in favor with the children in their new village."

"Father, I know you want them to increase in stature. Would you also please touch their bodies and heal them from asthma attacks?"

"Lord, help my grandchildren to continue to recognize you as their source and to choose the path that leads to your favor."

As she has prayed through the years, some of the most obvious requests generated by this Scripture were that her grandchildren might:

Increase in wisdom by
    not leaning on their own understanding.
    reading God's Word and memorizing Scriptures.
    gaining a gift of discernment.
    abhorring evil and clinging to good.
    making wise choices daily.
    seeking first the kingdom of God.

Increase in stature by
　seeking God's protection and provision.
　learning to eat healthy and exercise properly.
　determining never to abuse their bodies with drugs or alcohol.
　recognizing God as healer.

Increase in favor with God by
　developing a personal relationship with him at an early age.
　seeking him with all their hearts.
　obeying God's commands.
　loving those who are lost without the Savior.
　exhibiting the fruit of the Spirit.

Increase in favor with men by
　obeying their parents.
　respecting authority.
　developing a positive, encouraging personality.
　exhibiting compassion for the hurting.
　treating others as they want to be treated.

Building a Grandchild's Faith

Sometimes our grandchildren's spiritual growth is accelerated in unexpected ways on very ordinary days, as our next story illustrates.

When Grandmother Judy finally came home following surgery to remove a tumor on her brain, she had to lie very still. Her grandchildren would come into her room for brief visits, but she couldn't even turn her head to look at them.

Six-year-old Marshall wanted his Meemaw to be able to do something with him, so she suggested he go on a scavenger hunt like they often did together. "Take a basket and bring back things you find in the woods or on the lawn and tell me about them," she said. Then she asked him what he'd like to find on his hunt.

"A perfect arrowhead," he answered immediately.

"Then I'll pray you get your heart's desire," she told him, closing her eyes.

A couple of hours later he came back with his treasure. "You won't believe what God did, Meemaw!" he said excitedly. "Look! Not just one but two perfect arrowheads!"

He had been helping his grandfather landscape by clearing out some brush when he saw the first one. He inspected it carefully; sure enough, it was perfect. As far as his granddad knew, no one had ever found an arrowhead there before. Marshall went back and began raking leaves and debris in the same spot. There he pulled up his second arrowhead, unblemished by time or the elements. Then he showed his grandmother his other finds—feathers, pinecones, and unusual rocks.

"Marshall's faith grew tremendously that afternoon when he saw God answer a request he and his grandmother had prayed for," she said, "even something as impossible as finding exactly what he wanted on an afternoon scavenger hunt. He's twelve now and still keeps his two arrowheads in his small 'treasure box' as proof to an answer to prayer."

Grandmother Judy is well now, and she often takes Marshall on adventures beyond his beloved woods. They've traveled together on prayer journeys to foreign countries, where she has taught him more about how to pray for the nations of the world.

A Normal Way to Start the Day

Charlene says that since her grandchildren range in age over a twenty-year span, the specifics of what she prays for them are different. "Some common elements in my prayers have always been the same. For the little ones and the grade-school-age grandchildren, I pray about their personality development. For the teenagers, I pray about their future life partners and their careers. For the adults, I pray about their walk and ministry."

Whenever Grandma Charlene is with a grandchild overnight, she prays with her before they go to bed. "I always thank God for giving her to me for a grandchild, and for the relationship we have. I ask God to keep her in health, safety, and prosperity, to blind her eyes to temptation, and to cause her to get caught anytime she does something wrong. I ask the Father to fill this child with his Holy Spirit and the evidence of one or more of the fruits of the Spirit as a character trait. For example, 'Father, please fill Molly with your Holy Spirit, and help her to be kind and gentle with everyone.'

"I get up early in the morning to pray and read the Bible. That means when the grandchildren wake up and come out of their bedroom, I'm in my chair praying. They often snuggle up with me as I finish. I'll read a few verses or pray aloud while they are there so they learn this is the normal way to start the day."

A Concern for Teenagers' Faith

A recent survey shows that many teenagers have shocking misconceptions about Christianity and the truth of the Bible. All the more reason for grandparents to pray them through these turbulent years.

"Today's teens think they have learned and absorbed whatever the Christian faith has to offer and they are not questioning their spiritual beliefs," says researcher George Barna. "Among teenagers we will continue to get well-intentioned but misinformed faith perspectives that lead to bad choices and spiritual confusion. As they are the future leaders of the Christian church, we must be concerned about the substance of the faith that will be communicated and practiced in the long-term." Barna also says that "teens are more likely than adults to believe in salvation by good deeds, and to contend that Jesus was a sinner."[2]

The need to pray for the younger generation's spiritual development is self-evident. We want to help them understand that salvation comes only by faith in Christ and that it is possible because Jesus lived without sin and willingly died to pay for the sins of all who confess him as Savior.[3]

Our next story is an example of a teenager who strayed from the Lord. But later he realized that the faith of his grandmother—a faith he once had known—was missing from his life.

Kevin and his parents lived in Grandmother Eva's home for two years before he started school. Eva and his mother took him to church and taught him the ways of the Lord during those early years. When he reached his teens, Kevin dropped out of church except for occasional visits. But Grandmother Eva kept praying for him.

At age eighteen, Kevin saw for himself the power of prayer. His best friend's mother had suddenly lost consciousness while visiting friends. She was flown back to a hospital in her home city, but for more than a week, doctors could not diagnose the problem. When Kevin went to see her, he was quite shaken to find her lying so still and unresponsive. Then he dropped by Grandma Eva's house.

"Grandma, I need you to do something for me," he said, telling her about his concern. "Will you pray? If this was my mother, I wouldn't want her to be like this—and maybe die."

"Of course," Eva told him. "But I won't just pray about the situation by myself. I'll pray in agreement with you that God will restore your friend's mom to consciousness and that her family and caregivers will know God did it."

The two of them prayed together in her home, then Kevin returned to the hospital. Within one hour after he got there, the woman opened her eyes and asked where she was.

"This has made a lasting impression on my grandson!" Eva said. "He truly knows that God is the answer to our problems and that he responds to our prayers. I believe that when a child is trained in the way of the Lord, when he is old, he will not depart from it."

"Lord, Protect Them from Deception"

How do you relate to and pray for grandchildren being raised in a different religious stream? Grandmother Flo is dealing with this problem, since her daughter-in-law now takes her two sons to her own family's religious services, which Flo believes are not biblically based.

"We tell our teenaged grandsons our main concern is that they keep an ongoing personal relationship with Jesus, which they had as youngsters when they went to church with us," Flo told us. "I pray every day that God will keep them close to him and protect them from being deceived. We encourage the boys to keep up their prayer life. We also look for opportunities to share the love of God with them and let them know we're praying for them."

As our grandchildren grow up and are educated in this twenty-first century, they are subject to temptations and pressures we grandparents never encountered in our youth. It's important to pray they will be protected from deception. We can use this prayer from the Old Testament as a model, paraphrasing it for each grand-child:

> Jabez called on the God of Israel saying, "Oh, that You would bless me indeed, and enlarge my territory, that Your hand would be with me, and that You would keep me from evil, that I may not cause pain!" So God granted him what he requested.
>
> —1 Chronicles 4:10 NKJV

In his excellent book *The Prayer of Jabez*, Bruce Wilkinson talks about how weak our human wisdom is in confronting the enemy: "The nature of evil is to deceive us with a little bit of the truth—not all of it, mind you, but just enough to trick us. Adam and Eve weren't any more prone to succumb to temptation than we are. In fact, unlike us, they were perfect in every way, and none of their genuine needs were unmet. Satan approached the human race at its peak of promise and performance—and crushed us with one friendly conversation. That's why, like Jabez, we should pray for protection from deception."[4]

Grandmother's Influence for Change

Author Jay Kesler reminds us of an important spiritual principle: "We cannot give our grandchildren something which we do not possess. A life thoroughly committed to Christ, lived and tested over time, seasoned with experience and humility, is more powerful than most people ever imagine. Our backgrounds do affect us; we are the product of the blood in our veins. People who have a heritage of godly grandparents carry this influence into their lives sometimes without ever recognizing its source."[5]

Noreen's story illustrates how a grandparent can help to build self-esteem in a child and keep his spiritual life on an even keel. She was concerned when she heard her great-grandson, Troy, using curse words he had picked up from playing with older kids. He was the smallest in the group, so he used rough language to defend himself. When the other kids called him names and talked about how mean he was, he tried to live up to the tough image.

"You are not mean," Grandma Noreen said to him. "You are a good boy, and I love you." She expressed love for him when others put him down, and she prayed God would change him. As she affirmed and encouraged him at every opportunity, Troy believed what his great-grandma told him, and he began to reform.

"Now there's a special bond between us," Noreen said. "He gets along well with others, has a sweet nature, and excels in baseball. I have a 'good' little great-grandson who loves Jesus."

Without Noreen's prayers and positive input, Troy could easily have grown up to be an angry, rebellious teenager. But Noreen helped him to see that a right relationship with Jesus would enable him to form healthy friendships that aren't based on insecurity.

As dear as our grandchildren are to us, it's important to remember that God has no grandchildren—only children. Regardless of how godly a child's parents or grandparents may be, he or she must individually embrace the Christian faith. We can impact our grandchildren by modeling the Christian life before them—teaching by example—and by persisting in faithful prayer that each grandchild will receive Christ as Savior and Lord and become a positive influence among his or her peers.

Prayer

Lord, I pray that while my grandchildren are young they will accept Jesus as their Lord and will remain within the boundaries of his care. As they grow, help them develop godly character. May my grandchildren, like Jesus, increase in wisdom and stature and in favor with you and with men. Give them the qualities they will need to build their faith and to trust you in every area of their lives. I ask this in Jesus' name. Amen.

Helpful Scriptures

"I am the vine; you are the branches. If a man remains in me and I in him, he will bear much fruit; apart from me you can do nothing."

—John 15:5

And without faith it is impossible to please God, because anyone who comes to him must believe that he exists and that he rewards those who earnestly seek him.

—Hebrews 11:6

Everyone who calls on the name of the Lord will be saved.

—Acts 2:21

I urge, then . . . that requests, prayers, intercession and thanksgiving be made for everyone. . . . This is good, and pleases God our Savior, who wants all men to be saved and to come to a knowledge of the truth.

—1 Timothy 2:1, 3–4

Then little children were brought to Jesus for him to place his hands on them and pray for them. But the disciples rebuked those who brought them. Jesus said, "Let the little children come to me, and do not hinder them, for the kingdom of heaven belongs to such as these."

—Matthew 19:13–14

Scripture Prayer

Thank you, Lord, that you cherish little children. I present my grandchildren [names] to you today. Please reveal to them the truths of your kingdom, and keep them in your loving care [Matt. 19:13–14].

Related Scripture References

Romans 10:9–11
2 Peter 1:5–8; 3:8–9
1 John 1:9; 2:3–6, 28–29

chapter
3

Praying for Homes and families

We will tell the next generation the praiseworthy deeds of the LORD, his power, and the wonders he has done.... He commanded our forefathers to teach their children ... even the children yet to be born, and they in turn would tell their children. Then they would put their trust in God and would not forget his deeds but would keep his commands.

—Psalm 78:4–7

The family is the place where the deep understanding that people are significant, important, worthwhile, with a purpose in life, should be learned at an early age. The family is the place where children should learn that human beings have been made in the image of God and are therefore very special in the universe.

—Edith Schaeffer, *What Is a Family?*

*D*espite cultural changes and the diminishing of moral standards over the past decade, the family remains the building block of society. True, the profile of an "average family" may be different from that of our childhood. But the homes your grandchildren grow up

49

in are the incubators of the next generation. Those children and their parents or guardians can reap great blessings through the love and prayers of grandparents.

One survey declares, "Grandparents are living longer, and have shared lives across generations for longer than ever before. . . . They have greater intergenerational contact . . . [and] are becoming more important than at any time in American history."[1] Yet a different survey states, "The fragmentation of family structure, distance, divorce and the number of people having children later in life have increased the challenge of maintaining intergenerational ties."[2]

These societal changes mean that while our opportunities for influencing our grandchildren may be richer than ever before, we also have more barriers to overcome than did previous generations of grandparents. But our faith in God, love for our grandchildren, and diligence in prayer can help us find ways to overcome the barriers.

Never Underestimate the Power of Prayer

Perhaps your grandchildren are being raised in a Christian home, but sometimes that's not the case. Or maybe only one parent is a Christian, so the children receive conflicting messages about right and wrong. Whatever the environment, it can be transformed through the power of prayer, as Lorene's story illustrates.

When she learned that her daughter-in-law was taking three-year-old Jenny with her to the bar where she worked as a waitress, Lorene prayed even more diligently for the protection of her first grandchild. Though she had no legal right to intervene, this grandmother's strong faith in God motivated her to stand in the prayer gap for Jenny. She knew prayer could make a difference.

"For almost two years, I saw God's faithfulness to little Jenny as I prayed for her continually, asking him to keep her safe," Lorene wrote. "Now she is sixteen, has accepted Jesus as her Savior, and is living with my son and his second wife and family. She is doing well in school and is gaining self-confidence through performing with the drill team. It is possible to see circumstances change through prayer."

We can pray for peace in the home, for godly and loving parents, for good relationships among the siblings, for a home filled with God's love, for a neighborhood that is a safe and nurturing place. We can also ask God to provide positive role models for our grandchildren among friends, family members, and grandparents who live close by.

In some cases, a grandparent's prayers can help head off a crisis before it occurs. Gail learned the power of this truth when she received an anxious phone call at work early one morning. "Mom, the doctor wants me to have an amniocentesis done," her daughter said with panic in her voice. "The latest sonogram shows that something is wrong with the baby's head, and they want to run more tests. The doctor has even said I should consider an abortion if the problem turns out to be serious."

Gail immediately began to pray and felt the Holy Spirit instructing her that her daughter and son-in-law should be prayed for before going in for the test.

"At the time, my son-in-law was not a Christian and was reluctant to accept personal prayer," Gail said. "But he finally agreed, and our pastor met them at the church, where he prayed for my daughter and the baby. And God intervened! There were no further serious problems, and the baby was born perfectly normal. We should never underestimate the power of prayer."

Praying for Restoration

Sally and Don adopted their daughter, Shawna, when she was six weeks old. Doctors said she had "failure to thrive" syndrome because she had lived in a foster home for her first six weeks and that she was underweight from lack of desire to eat. Whatever the reason, she never seemed to bond adequately with her adoptive parents, who had difficulties with her throughout her childhood.

At age nineteen Shawna got pregnant and decided to keep Cody after he was born. Sally and Don made a special place in their hearts and home for their only grandson. Shawna resolved to marry the baby's father and planned a big wedding, but she canceled it three weeks before the date. Then two months later they got married before a judge. Within a few weeks they were separated, as Shawna's drinking problem spun out of control, and soon they divorced. The judge gave her custody of Cody, provided she stayed at her parents' home so they could help rear him.

Shawna went to her job each morning, leaving the baby with her parents. Sally fed and dressed him before leaving for her teaching job, and Don took him to day care every morning. In the afternoons, Don's parents kept him. He was a happy, well-adjusted baby with both his grandparents and his great-grandparents caring for him.

When Cody was barely two, Shawna moved in with the baby's father. "God convicted me that I needed to do everything I could to help their relationship work," Sally said. "Don and I had thought seriously of trying to adopt Cody to give him a stable home, but the Lord showed us we had to let him go with Shawna. We could only pray for his parents to provide the kind of home he needed. We encouraged our daughter to take responsibility for her own life and urged her to go to an alcoholism support group."

The uncertainty and stress continue. But the grandparents stay in touch, take care of Cody when he's sick, and make sure he's safe. He once told Sally his parents "talk loud" to each other, and that at such times his mother tells him it's his "hush time," meaning he must get out of the way and be quiet.

Can this marriage be restored? Sally and Don continue to pray that it will, for that would be best for their grandson. And they know it is possible with wise counseling and a willingness from both parties to allow God's love to change their hearts.

"As much heartache as we've been through with our Shawna and Cody, I wouldn't take anything for what it has taught me," Sally said. "I realize what other seemingly 'normal' families are going through behind closed doors. I love my little grandson and pray for God's best for him. I also love my daughter and pray she will achieve her potential. I really want this family to make it, and that's saying a lot, considering the way I once felt about the situation. I am praying they will become a testimony of God's grace."

Staying Connected

Ways you can stay connected with your grandchildren and their families:

Let them know you pray for them regularly, and invite them to share prayer requests with you. Communicating by e-mail is a good way to do this if you have a computer.

If geographical locations allow, plan activities—maybe special dinners or picnics—that include all the grandchildren and their parents.

Plan short excursions, weekend trips, or activities at home when you can have individual time with each grandchild.

Volunteer to play games with your grandchildren, and look for opportunities to teach them about good sportsmanship.

Children love to receive mail! Send your grandchildren postcards when you are traveling, and write them notes of encouragement often, even if they live in your town. Letters and cards can be keepsakes for them to read over and over.

Teach them a skill that perhaps parents don't have time for, such as cooking, knitting, sewing, painting, gardening.

Help them with a project, such as making a family scrapbook, organizing their collection of special treasures, creating their own prayer journal.

Help them shop for or create special-occasion gifts for their parents or siblings.

As often as possible, attend their games or performances.

Daily Prayer Reminders

Grammy and Papa in Alabama pray daily for their natural grandson, Ralph, and two preschool stepgrandchildren. Ever since he was small, they've kept Ralph's picture on their refrigerator with Scripture verses underneath, which they pray for him every day. Often they change the verse to address a particular need. Since his parents' divorce, they see him less and less and are particularly concerned about his lack of spiritual training. Primarily they pray for the protection of all three grandchildren, asking the Lord to keep them from ungodly influences, especially through television. They also pray that God's Word will be planted in their hearts.

Merrie and her husband keep pictures of their three grandchildren tucked in the bowl of fresh fruit on their dining table. "Every morning after breakfast, we take these pictures from the fruit bowl and pray over them," she said. "This symbolizes that we want the fruit of the Spirit to be manifested in their lives. We pray specifically for their character traits to be developed each day, as well as for God's intervention in any special needs they may have."

Praying for a Son and His Descendants

Shortly after Bet became a Christian some thirty years ago, the following verse seemed to spring to life for her: "They shall not labor in vain, or bear children for calamity; for they are the offspring of those blessed by the LORD, and their descendants with them" (Isa. 65:23 NASB).

"Our three sons were teenagers at the time," she said. "Several months after receiving this promise from God, we discovered our oldest son, sixteen-year-old Pete, was a drug addict. Over the next few years as we walked with him through drug rehabilitation programs, I would read this Scripture in times of discouragement. Then I would pray, 'O, Lord, this is such a calamity. And your Word says I did not bear children for calamity.'"

One day as Bet was praying this verse again, she felt the Holy Spirit whisper to her, *This is not a calamity. Not knowing Jesus*

Christ is a calamity. From that time on, God gave her faith to believe him for the salvation of all three of their sons and for their descendants yet to be born.

Years passed. When Pete, now fully recovered, got married, Bet gave the couple a beautiful leather-bound Bible as a wedding gift, although neither Pete nor his fiancée were Christians at the time. Inside she marked the text of Isaiah 65:23.

"Five years later, they were expecting our first grandchild," Bet said. "Pete's wife was having trouble in delivery, and the doctor wanted to do a C-section because the baby was in a breech position. Pete came out into the hospital hallway where we were waiting and asked his dad and me to pray that God would turn the baby. Several of us stood in a circle and prayed, asking God to be merciful. Even as we prayed, the baby turned in her mother's womb."

Moments later a nurse called Pete to come into the birthing room if he wanted to see his baby being born. Bet's granddaughter was born beautiful and healthy.

"Later, Pete told me that after Susan's birth, he began to read the Bible I had given him for a wedding gift," Bet told us. "He was excited to see that I had marked Isaiah 65:23 and had written in the margin the date I had claimed my descendants for the Lord. Susan was born sixteen years later to the day! God has been faithful to his Word. All our sons have come to the Lord, and several of our grandchildren, including twelve-year-old Susan. When God gives you a promise, hold onto it."

Bet learned to pray first for her children and now is better equipped to pray for her grandchildren and their homes and families.[3]

Prayer Unites a Family

From the time her girls were tiny, Josie and her husband, Ralph, prayed for their daughters' future mates and for every aspect of their lives. Imagine their chagrin when sixteen-year-old Amber began dating Dean, a pig farmer who was eight years older than she. But the romance blossomed, and in time, they gave Amber and Dean their blessing to marry. After starting off well, the marriage hit rock bottom within a year, as Dean turned out to be a controlling husband and a substance abuser.

The day they helped Amber move out was a heartache for Josie. "I knew separation was necessary for the sanity and safety of my daughter," she recalled. "But I was so hoping it wouldn't end in divorce. I prayed, 'Lord, my husband and I made a covenant with you, a covenant of love and faith for our daughters and their spouses. I remind you that ever since Amber was a baby, I've prayed for her husband, and I'm not giving up on him. Please, Lord, reveal your love to Dean. Let him meet you face to face. I know you can save him, and you can save this marriage.'"

One evening Amber called with startling news. "Mom, Dean went out to the woods today, fell flat on his face, and gave his heart to Jesus. He sounds very repentant for what he's done, and he's asked my forgiveness. He wants me back."

"Well, we didn't move you out for you to stay where you are forever," Josie responded. "If you feel God is in this, move back in with him, honey."

After that day in the woods with God, Dean grew in his Christian faith through prayer, godly mentoring, and biblical teaching. His marriage became Christ centered, and eventually he and Amber had four children. Josie and Ralph are intercessors who travel the world, and Dean has become their key prayer person.

Once when Josie and Ralph were in Israel leading a prayer tour, Josie felt the urge to go home a day early. Then she got word that Dean, now forty-two, was having chest pains, and called her group together to pray.

At that very hour back in Atlanta, Dean, who was on a six-lane freeway driving himself to the doctor, had a heart attack. Praying he could keep control of his truck and not hurt anyone, Dean pulled off the freeway and parked behind a building, then fell out of the vehicle. Someone saw him, called an ambulance, and they rushed him to a hospital just one block away. A heart specialist immediately operated on him to open the 100 percent blockage in an artery.

When the hospital called to alert Amber that Dean was undergoing heart surgery, their fifteen-year-old daughter, Megan, took the call. Ever the cool, levelheaded one, she began praying for her dad's complete recovery with an unshakable faith that God was in control. She quickly packed a bag for her mother, and when Amber walked into the house, she calmly told her the news.

Amber headed for the hospital while Megan stayed with the three younger children. As twelve-year-old Michael was praying for his dad, he drew a picture of him in the hospital with four angels surrounding his bed. Underneath he wrote, "My dad will live and not die."

Four days after surgery, Dean came home, and Josie went to be with him and his family. He returned to his job just two weeks later. "His quick recovery truly was a miracle, and we thank God for it," Josie said. "I again reminded God of our covenant of love and faith for our daughter's family; I didn't want my grandchildren to grow up without a father. I pray daily for all seven of my grandchildren and take each of them on a prayer journey with me whenever I can. All of them are learning the power of prayer."

Staying Connected with Grandchildren

Many involved grandparents like Josie and Ralph are taking their grandchildren on such prayer journeys, or on short vacations, to provide opportunities for bonding. Some plan "cousins only" trips or camping expeditions for those over a certain age. Others make a once-a-year visit to baby-sit so the parents can have a few days' getaway without the children. Or they stay in touch with grandchildren by recording audiocassettes of themselves reading a story or singing silly songs.

When their grandchildren were young, Dorothy and Charles began a tradition of taking two cousins with them on a vacation every year. The grandparents let the kids participate in deciding where to go. With an aim to making the trips both fun and educational, Dorothy and Charles asked each child to write a brief report about the things they experienced on the excursion. It took several years for all eleven grandchildren—who are now teenagers or young adults—to have their turn.

Recently, for Dorothy's eightieth birthday, Charles compiled an "I remember" book to mark the occasion. All the grandchildren wrote about the vacation trips they had enjoyed with "Do-Lolly" and "Do-Daddy" and the wonderful memories they cherish from those adventures.

One grandmother regularly sends recordings to her four grandchildren living overseas. She will read an entire book to them, then pray for them. "They feel closer to me when they can hear my voice, so I try to send them tapes frequently," she said. "I'm constantly searching for the right book for each child's specific age. Their mom tells me they often go to sleep at night listening to my story and prayer for them."

Passing on a Heritage through Prayer

I (Quin) am thrilled by this verse: "Know therefore that the LORD your God is God; he is the faithful God, keeping his covenant of love to a thousand generations of those who love him and keep his commands" (Deut. 7:9).

What an inheritance! And what a privilege to pass on to our children and grandchildren the greatest heritage possible—the example of our prayer lives, after which they can model their own. Whenever I have the opportunity to hold one of our grandchildren in my lap, I talk to him or her about God's plan for his or her future. One tradition in our family is a yearly "blessing ceremony," when all our grandchildren come to a party to be prayed over by their granddad and me. Patiently they wait in line for their blessing to be bestowed, followed by refreshments and play.

I've watched my adult children almost outdistance me in prayer in recent years. Since becoming parents, they've learned the importance of praying earnestly for the little ones God has entrusted to them. Together, we grandparents and parents are teaching these children to pray. For one thing, they hear us pray aloud for them often, in everyday situations, not just at the table or at bedtime. And they're catching on.

Once when Lyden and his Papa LeRoy were in the back yard playing softball, LeRoy injured his fingers trying to catch a ball the three-year-old had whopped across the fence. Lyden quickly grabbed his granddad's bruised hand and prayed, "Jesus, please heal his hurt. Amen."

Through our prayers, our grandchildren can become power-houses to change the world in every field of work. Strengthened by the Holy Spirit and supported by our prayers, our children's children can influence an ungodly world—revealing Christ to their fellow students, teachers, or workmates—and be salt and light to their generation. Only God knows what will happen if we truly pray for our children and grandchildren, leaving footprints of faith for them to follow.[4]

Quin's Specific Prayers

While I join my prayers with my grandchildren's parents, I also pray specific prayers daily for all my grandchildren. My main Scrip-ture prayer is that "the Spirit of the Lord will rest on my grand-children—the Spirit of wisdom and of understanding, the Spirit of counsel and of power, the Spirit of knowledge and the [rever-ential] fear of the Lord" (Isa. 11:2). But I add practical prayers as I see needs in their lives or when their parents share concerns they want covered in prayer. Here's how I am currently praying.

For Kara, six, in first grade: "Lord, I pray for her to gain some like-minded friends who love you as passionately as she does. I thank you for her above-average academic skills and ask that she continue to be challenged to excel. Lord, may she always have a quick mind and a deep hunger for knowledge with the ability to apply it wisely in her life. Lord, help her to continue to develop good leadership qualities."

For Lyden, five, in kindergarten: "I pray for his eye and hand coordination to improve so he will be able to write what he is hearing and learning. I thank you, God, for his sweet personality, his sports ability, and his computer skills to perform his phonics lessons. I pray for him to develop better eating habits. Lord, I pray you will help him to gain some Christian 'best buddies' who will encourage him in his faith. Thank you that he enjoys Bible stories, building things, playing softball, and sleeping over at his grandmother's house."

For Evangeline, four, in preschool: "Lord, I pray for her to achieve a substantial weight gain as she is undersize. Help her to eat right and exercise. I pray for her to mature and develop good social skills. I pray for the right school program to help her. Thank you, God, for her quick smile, artistic ability, and love for her new baby brother. I'm grateful for the special love she has for you and her Bible books."

For Victoria Jewett, four, in preschool: "I pray for her health to improve immensely, and for her to be protected from respiratory illnesses. Lord, I pray you will help her to be able to speak more clearly and that she will make some special friends. I pray she will continue to do well in her gymnastics class without getting injured. Thank you, Lord, for her ability to do things well with her hands, for her love for cooking and dolls and pretty clothes, especially pink."

For Samuel, four, in preschool: "Lord, please help him to adjust well to his new home and Christian preschool and to make lots of wholesome friends. Thank you, Lord, for his excellent vocabulary, his love of singing, his creativity, his mechanical ability, and his grasp of the Bible."

For Ethan, three months, in the crib: "Lord, thank you for this newest grandchild who is so alert and curious. Thank you for his Christian parents, who will bring him up in the ways of the Lord. Give them wisdom as they raise this their first son. I pray he will continue to have a sweet and quiet spirit. Lord, protect him from serious childhood diseases. As he matures, I pray he will make an early decision to follow Christ as his siblings and cousins have already chosen to do."

Quin's Mom's Legacy of Love

When my mother sold her boardinghouse in Tallahassee, she bought some rental cottages on the sound in the fishing village of

Destin, Florida, where my three children loved to visit her. They could dive off her dock, swim across to Holiday Island, or go with her to the nearby Gulf of Mexico for a romp in the waves. They collected shells and cooked crabs and went fishing in the little pools all around her place.

But it wasn't all play. When work was involved, she made it fun, too, working alongside them. They learned how to book reservations for the cottages over the phone, how to rent them out, and how to help her clean them after the guests checked out. She taught my youngsters safety rules, expected them to obey when she spoke, and rewarded them with privileges that far outshone what we could have done for them.

Grandchildren were to be enjoyed and loved, she said. She firmly believed the Scripture which declares, "Children's children are a crown to the aged" (Prov. 17:6). When our three came back home to us, they talked nonstop about their adventures and admitted they shared some special secrets with her.

She'd sing with them, read to them, and let them sit up late studying the stars. She'd even recite the "elocution" pieces she had learned as a girl in high school—poetry and essays she still remembered from the 1920s.

As my children grew older, they called her for prayer whenever they were facing a hard time—a test in school, a financial setback, a broken relationship—and she would respond by praying with them on the phone. Sometimes when I was with her during her "prayer closet" time, she would raise her hands to heaven and say aloud, "Lord, these ten fingers represent my ten grandchildren. Now I bring them before your throne to pray for them," and she'd pray specifically for each one's needs that day.

Mom died a few weeks before my son graduated from college. At his graduation he looked heavenward and said, "How I wish Mother Jewett could be here today to see me receive this diploma. She helped me earn it with her prayers." We all shed a few tears, remembering.[5]

My younger daughter, Sherry, wrote of her, "What I most remember and treasure about my grandmother was her unconditional love for me. She accepted me just like I was and never tried to change me. I spent many happy summers with her and remember her famous cooking—fried chicken, hush puppies, and cinnamon rolls. Her laugh and helpful counsel blessed so many people. A wise businesswoman, Mother Jewett invested in land, but most of all she invested in me and showed the love of the heavenly Father to me."

Wise grandparents leave a lifelong impression when they bestow love.

Prayer

Lord, I pray for peace in the environment in which my grandchildren are reared. May it be a home filled with your love and be a neighborhood that is safe. I pray you will give their parents or guardians the wisdom and understanding to nurture them. Also provide them positive role models who will be godly examples. Thank you for the gift of these precious children. Amen.

Helpful Scriptures

Children, obey your parents in the Lord, for this is right. "Honor your father and mother"—which is the first commandment with a promise—"that it may go well with you and that you may enjoy long life on the earth." Fathers, do not exasperate your children; instead, bring them up in the training and instruction of the Lord.

—Ephesians 6:1–4

Dear children, let us not love with words or tongue but with actions and in truth.

—1 John 3:18

My people will live in peaceful dwelling places, in secure homes, in undisturbed places of rest.

—Isaiah 32:18

Scripture Prayer

Thank you, Lord, that you will turn the hearts of the fathers of my grandchildren [names] toward them. And that you will turn my grandchildren's hearts toward their fathers [Mal. 4:6]. Lord, I trust you to bring any healing that's needed into these relationships and to strengthen the bonds of love in this family.

Related Scripture References

Psalms 37:1–9; 68:4–6; 133
Philippians 2:3–5

Praying for friends and Schooling

The child grew and became strong; he was filled with wisdom, and the grace of God was upon him.... Jesus grew
in wisdom and stature, and in favor with God and men.

—Luke 2:40, 52

*Jumping in with good advice is our natural reaction to any
problem our grandchildren have. But resisting the urge to
shower them with the benefit of our great wisdom is the sign
of a good listener.... Provide a safe place where they can
come and share their joys and their sorrows, their fears, fail-
ures, and successes, knowing you are there to hear their
every word.*

—Jan Stoop and Betty Southard,
The Grandmother Book

Friends and schooling are two areas in which grandchildren need
our prayers far more than we may realize. These two elements—
their peers and their education—probably impact children more
than any other, except for the influence of home and family.
Besides providing prayer support during these formative years, we

can also be compassionate listeners as they share their problems, hopes, and dreams.

Every child yearns to have a best friend. But it's important to pray that the friends your grandchildren already have will be a positive influence on them, and vice versa. Also pray that from among their acquaintances, your grandchildren will form closer ties with the ones who will strengthen their relationship with God, rather than weaken it. Sometimes a grandmother has a unique opportunity to help a grandchild feel accepted among his peers. The following story is an example.

"I Can Help You"

Our friend Sharon noticed, while attending a skating birthday party for one of her six grandchildren, that eleven-year-old Blake was missing out on a good time. It appeared that all the kids at the party were skating except him. He helped some of the others find a pair of skates in their size; then he started helping with the refreshments.

"Honey, you'd better get out there and enjoy the fun before the party's over," she told him. "Where are your skates?"

"Oh, Mums, I don't feel like skating," he answered. "My leg hurts."

A little while later, Blake's dad arrived. "What has happened to Blake's leg so that he can't go skating?" she asked her son, thinking the child had been hurt in an accident.

"There's nothing wrong with his leg, Mom," her son said with a chuckle. "He doesn't know how to skate."

Suddenly Sharon decided to step in and do the job herself, even though she had not been on skates for more than thirty years. Sitting down next to Blake, she put her arm around him and said, "Sweetheart, Mums knows how to skate, and I can help you learn how. You want to try?"

"Okay," he said.

Sharon bought a pair of socks at the service counter, then found skates in their sizes. They both wobbled a bit as they ventured onto the floor, but Sharon soon got her footing and gave Blake tips on how to keep his balance as they moved slowly around the edge of the rink.

"Hey, Mums! This is cool!" Blake shouted over the music as they started their third lap. But then he got distracted and lost his balance. As they tried to leave the floor, Blake fell, taking Sharon with him. The force of the fall crushed the bone just above her left wrist, so she finished the party in the emergency room.

After she'd left the building, Blake turned to Sharon's daughter-in-law and said, "Mom, I'm so sorry Mums hurt herself, but I'm going to go around one more time." He took off and hasn't missed a chance to go skating since.

"My husband couldn't believe it when he found out what had happened," Sharon said. "He'd never seen me on skates before and thought it was a foolish thing for me to do. But I was concerned that my grandson was missing the fun with the other kids, and it was worth it to see him get in the middle of all the activity. It never occurred to me that I was taking a risk.

"I prayed Blake wouldn't suffer with guilt and feel it was his fault that I got hurt, but that wasn't a problem. Learning to skate has been a healthy energy outlet for him, and he feels more accepted by his friends and peers. The experience did create a special bond between us, though, and that's a bonus I appreciate. Blake is my oldest grandchild and is really special to me. I'm quite sure God has his hand on this boy."

Substitute Grandmothers Needed

Tammy recently told us that although most of her friends have their children in Christian schools, she feels God has led her to keep her four in public schools. However, that may mean they'll face considerable challenges and have opportunities to wander from what Tammy has taught them.

"My fourteen-year-old twin boys still come to me to talk through the issues they confront," she said. "I hope they always will. My younger two are in elementary school and don't have as much peer pressure. But since their grandparents don't live close by, I've enlisted some older women in our church as substitute grandmas to pray for my four children. I pray daily that they will be strong witnesses for Christ and good examples to their classmates. I've asked their surrogate grandmas to pray that, too, as well as anything else the Lord shows them about my children's needs or weaknesses."

Tammy says her children's closest friends are the ones they've made through church activities. She encourages these relationships by letting her kids invite their friends for sleepovers, skating parties, and picnics at the park.

Even good children can be led astray, especially in our culture where many working parents find it difficult to spend as much time as they would like with their children. In such cases, peer influence becomes much stronger and prayer a higher priority. "Lord, protect our grandchildren from evil companions" is a continual prayer of one grandmother.

You may occasionally become aware that your grandchild's peers are having a negative influence on him. Of course you should commit to pray about the situation. But also you can pray for the right opportunity to say something like, "Grandson, be careful about making friends with people who pull you away from God, rather than drawing you closer to him. Sometimes those who appear to be your friends actually are the ones who can cause trouble in your life."

Remembering Answered Prayers

When facing discouragement about a grandchild's friends or school, we can recall how God answered prayers for our own children, and it challenges us to pray more specifically for our grandchildren. I (Quin) was encouraged as I thought back to the day our oldest child, Quinett, left to attend college hundreds of miles from home. I started praying for the school—the faculty, students, even the friends she'd make. Most of all, I prayed that many students would come to know Christ on that campus. Over the next three years, I didn't hear any reports that those prayers were answered.

But in her senior year, her brother, Keith, transferred to that college. That year, Bible studies had started up in several dorms, and Keith was attending one. Later he brought the two Bible study leaders to visit our home in the piney woods of Florida for a weekend. I got excited when they told me they had transferred to that college just so they could reach others for the Lord Jesus. Even the campus athletes were attending special Bible classes they had tailored to their needs.

"You two are an answer to my prayer," I said as I dished up their supper.

Maybe you will want to remember a time when you saw God move on behalf of your child in the areas of friends or school, and in the remembering, know better how to pray for your grandchild.

This year my oldest grandson, Lyden, started public school kindergarten after two years in a Christian preschool. I was concerned about the adverse influences he might find. I began praying that he'd have a teacher who would understand him and that he would make some new, supportive friends.

One of the reasons I think grandmas should go to schools to meet teachers and their grandchildren's friends is to have a better picture of how to pray for them. Seeing them in the classroom—where they sit, how they react to other students and their teachers—gives us a close-up look at what their everyday lives are like.

I was happy to learn that Lyden's teacher is a Christian, and she is thrilled that one of her students, his mother, and his grandmother pray every morning for her and her class. She gives him extra hugs when she knows someone has teased him over his drawing because he can't hold a pencil as well as the others. He's the youngest in the class, but he tries hard, and that counts with her. As for his meeting some like-minded friends, he has met some neat ones through his Sunday school class.

I've made it a point to meet each of my grandchildren's teachers and let them know I'm praying for them. I send them cards and gifts at Christmastime and never miss my grandchildren's class performances if I'm in town. I also take time to thank the teachers for their interest in my grandchildren. By supporting them, I feel I can encourage my grandchildren to respect and honor them. And I also pray they will encourage the children to develop their talents.

Some grandparents try to get to know their grandchildren's teachers whether they live close by or not. Grandma Belle lives hundreds of miles from her grandchildren, but whenever she visits them, she spends one day at school with each child.

Grandma Mitzi, who lives in the same town as her grandchildren, eats lunch with her second-grader every Friday in the school cafeteria. The kids in the class call her Grandma Mitzi, and they love the stories she tells when the teacher invites her to share.

Starting school or switching to a new school can be a traumatic adjustment for some children. After classes opened in the fall, eight-year-old Jody was getting sick every day, so her parents shared their concern with Grandma and Grandpa. Together they prayed over her, asking God to take away her anxiety and to help her eat normally. Within a week, her apprehensions diminished. She finally adjusted to her new classroom situation and was no longer sick.

Proactive Praying

Escalating incidents of deadly school violence have spawned fear in the hearts of parents and grandparents, as well as of children. Today's children are growing up in a vastly different and far more dangerous world than the one we knew when we were raising our own. But getting mired in hopelessness or denial is not the answer. We can be proactive through praying regularly for our schoolchildren, for their teachers and administrators, and for the community.

Increasing numbers of parents today are choosing to home-school their children, feeling it protects them from potential violence and ungodly teaching and sidesteps the problem of costly private school education. As young parents take up this challenge, grandparents' prayers are needed for encouragement and support.

My (Ruthanne's) younger stepdaughter, Melody, is home-schooling her three, who are in stairsteps two years apart. The challenges seem more daunting as they advance through the grades, and she's already wondering how she'll handle their high school studies. "Sometimes I wonder if it's the right thing," she says. "But then I turn on the TV or pick up the newspaper and think our way is really not bad, considering the alternatives."

While we were writing this book, a fatal shooting incident took place at a high school in California. Within days, dozens of copycat incidents were reported around the country. In Melody's city, a six-year-old child took a gun to school, and the parents were charged with child endangerment for having kept the gun within easy reach of a child. No wonder parents are concerned for their children's safety when they send them off to school.

John and I try to provide our daughter with as much encouragement and prayer support as we can, although we're twelve hundred miles away. The current prayer request is for Rachel, Lydia, and Joel to make friends through their church contacts or other outside activities. They had been members of a homeschoolers' "co-op" for extras such as art, music, dance, and science lab, but the hectic schedule left little time for forming friendships. Now Melody and three other moms have formed a group of home-schoolers to get together strictly for social outings and fun activities, and we're praying this group will expand and provide good friendship opportunities for the children.

An Adventure with Grandma

Sarah's granddaughter, seventeen-year-old Noel, slipped into depression after her mom decided to homeschool her and her younger sister. The family lived in a lovely location, but it was far from town. The four hours spent daily to drive the girls to and from a Christian school had been taking a toll on the family's nerves and schedule, so homeschooling was the parents' solution. But Noel missed her friends, felt lonely, and began sleeping in a large walk-in closet instead of in her bed.

Grandmother Sarah, who lives several hundred miles away, grew extremely concerned when she learned that Noel wasn't shaking off her depression. She asked God to show her what she could do to help. Noel and her sister are her only grandchildren, so they've been Sarah's special prayer project since they were born. She felt God gave her the idea that a change of scenery would help Noel.

After clearing the plan with the girl's parents, Sarah called her on the phone. "Hey, honey, how would you like to go on an adventure with me?" she asked exuberantly. "We could visit our relatives in Louisiana and Mississippi, tour some art museums, and go out to eat in fun restaurants."

Noel liked the idea, so they picked a date. They spent the first week in New Orleans, where a boy cousin took them on tours of the French Quarter and to out-of-the-way restaurants. He was particulary kind to Noel, making her feel very special. A favorite uncle and his wife flew in from St. Louis to visit them. Noel, a budding artist, enjoyed spending time in the art museums. Staying together in a motel that week gave Sarah and her granddaughter lots of time to talk about her dreams, which gave the grandmother new insights on how to pray more specifically for her. The second week, they drove to Mississippi to visit other relatives.

By the end of their fifteen-day adventure, Noel was no longer in depression. In fact, she was happy to get back to her homeschool classroom with her sister, and she resumed sleeping in her bed. She took new interest in her private art lessons, and soon some of her art was accepted for display in the student exhibit at a nearby museum.

Sarah prays many Scripture prayers for both her granddaughters. For example, she was impressed with a verse from the story of Daniel and the three young Hebrew men who were in exile in Babylon being prepared for the king's service. Sarah took note of this verse: "But Daniel resolved not to defile himself" (Dan. 1:8). Now she is praying that her granddaughters will choose not to defile themselves with darkness of any kind—immoral behavior, occult activity, or anything contrary to God's Word.

A Special Prayer Challenge

I (Ruthanne) remember when my stepdaughter, Linda, faced the challenge of finding a suitable school for her daughter. Amanda, our oldest grandchild, had attended public schools through the tenth grade, but drugs and gangs were a growing problem at her high school, and we were increasingly concerned for her safety. Also, she wanted to move to a better school to increase her chances of getting into a good college. But the best choice for a private school was more than an hour's drive away from the California town where they lived.

As we prayed about the matter, it seemed the best solution was for Linda to sell the house and find a place to rent reasonably close to her job and close enough for Amanda to drive to the private school. Linda's husband had died suddenly a few years before, and she needed to sell the large house anyway, as it was a financial burden to her. Although the real estate market had gone into a slump, she put the house up for sale and started looking for a house to rent. Amanda applied for admission and a scholarship to the private school, and we prayed for a miracle.

Toward the end of that summer, I flew to California to help Linda pack and get ready to move. Amanda had been accepted at the school and had been approved for a partial scholarship. Linda had a potential buyer for the house, though the couple's financial stability seemed a bit shaky, but she still hadn't found a suitable place to rent. I made the trip anyway, as it was the only time I was going to have for quite a while.

I arrived to find them pretty discouraged. The next day, all three of us checked on a few rentals, but none of them filled the bill. Then we drove to one last house before heading home.

"It's perfect!" I said when I saw the place, and they agreed. It was in a nice neighborhood, just the right size, with big trees, a fenced yard for the dog, and a closed garage. The problem was, thirty other families had already applied to rent this house. The owner, Mr. Smith, happened to be there when we arrived. He showed us around, gave Linda a form to complete, and asked her to leave it in the mailbox by eight o'clock that evening. Then he and members of his family would meet, review all the applications, and make their choice.

As soon as we got home, Linda filled out the form and gathered back-up documents. "Why don't you write a cover letter explaining why it's important for you to live there so Amanda will be close enough to drive to her new school?" I suggested. So Linda wrote a detailed letter about their dilemma and offered to pay a higher security deposit because of the dog. She even enclosed a picture of Amanda's schnauzer.

When they left to return the application, I unloaded the china cupboard onto the dining room table and began wrapping and packing glasses and china while praying furiously for God to give them favor with Mr. Smith. When they got back a couple of hours later, Linda was shocked to see her china cupboard empty and boxes stacked against the wall. "What are you doing?" she exclaimed.

"I'm packing boxes, and you gals are moving!" I told her confidently. "I just believe God is going to work this out so you can rent that house and sell this one." For the rest of the weekend, we sorted stuff, wrapped dishes, and packed, labeled, and taped boxes. You can imagine the shout of joy that went up when Mr. Smith called a few days later to say the house was theirs. He refused Linda's offer to pay a higher security deposit, and she found out later he had never even checked her references. He simply felt these two were the right people for the house.

They moved in time for Amanda to start her junior year at the private school, and the sale of the big house finally went through. Amanda excelled in her studies and was the pride of all her teachers. She won scholarships to three different colleges offering studies in her chosen field and was able to pick the one she wanted. Six years after that whirlwind move, Linda and I sat together to watch Amanda graduate with high honors and receive her degree in English and art history. When she walked across the stage, both of us burst into tears.

"All of us together, with God, did this," I told Linda, laughing and crying as we hugged one another. I was so glad my grandmother prayers—and the faith God gave me as I prayed—had been a part of the victory.

New Friends in Response to Prayer

A couple of years ago when I (Quin) visited one of my prayer partners in Texas, Becky shared her concern about her granddaughter who had been out of college for a couple of years. Jewel was overweight, lonely, and seemed to have no friends. That afternoon in a little lakeside cottage, the two of us prayed in agreement that God would give Jewel some special friends.

A couple of years later, as Becky and I were visiting on the phone, I asked, "By the way, did Jewel ever get any friends?"

"Did she ever!" Becky exclaimed. "She got so many friends she didn't know what to do with all of them. She lost weight, went to Uzbekistan for a year as a short-term missionary, and there met a young Christian man whom she plans to marry. Since I had a big part in raising this grandchild, my deepest concern is for God's best for her, including her choice of a husband. It's hard to see her marry someone from another country, but I'm praying for God's will to be done."

Like so many other praying grandmothers, she prays; she trusts; she waits. That's what grandmothers do!

When Karen, a first-grader, was having problems meeting Christian friends in public school, her parents alerted Grandma Beverly to join them in praying about the situation. A few schoolmates had tried to get close to Karen, but they seemed to have rather questionable family values. One little girl who wanted to be her friend recently told Karen her dad had gotten some body piercings, and went on to talk about the fun her family has playing computer games together. The games she named all contain occultic material.

Upon hearing this report, Grandma Beverly and the rest of the family prayed even harder that God would intervene. A short time later, a first-grader from another class whom Karen met during recess invited her to go to her church on a Wednesday evening for

Helpful Guidelines

Here are some helpful guidelines for praying for your grandchildren's friends and schooling:

Find out the names of your grandchildren's closest friends so you can pray for them by name. Pray your grandchildren will make friends with those who are courteous, trustworthy, honest, and helpful and that they and their friends will have a godly influence on one another.

Invite your grandchildren to share prayer requests with you concerning their friends or their friends' families. Ask your grandchildren to agree with you in prayer for these needs.

If you live near your grandchildren, invite them to visit your home with their friends for a picnic, to watch a special video, or for some other fun activity.

Take an interest in your grandchildren's schoolwork, assuring them that you're praying for them in areas in which they're struggling. Offer to help them with homework, if that's feasible, or offer to help them research a topic they're writing a report on.

Attend open house and other special events at their schools, and try to meet as many of their teachers as possible.

For gift-giving occasions, look for books and items related to activities or areas of study they are especially interested in. When you see a newspaper or magazine article you think they'll enjoy, mail it to them. These actions say to the child, "Grandma knows the things I like; she really cares about me."

Offer generous praise for their every achievement in sports, music, language clubs, school activities, academics, volunteer work, Bible memorization, and so on. As often as possible, attend their games or performances. Let them know you're praying for them in these endeavors, not that they will win every competition but that they will always do their best.

a special children's program. When Karen went—even though it's not the church her family regularly attends—she liked the program and enjoyed her new friend. Now it's a regular weekly activity, and the two sets of parents take turns driving the girls on Wednesday evenings. The first-graders can play together during recess at school, and they've already had sleepovers at one another's homes.

Preventing Dropouts

How many times have we read reports about young people with poor performances in school and low self-esteem getting in trouble with the law? Often they are easy prey for gangs, occult groups, or drug dealers simply because that's where they find the acceptance they're seeking. Our prayers can accomplish much to protect them from these negative elements. And we can reinforce our prayers by mentoring and tutoring our grandchildren, as well as other young people who have no grandmother figure in their lives.

One grandmother wrote, "Many children have difficulty understanding their teachers, and thus get behind in school. Some youngsters just barely get by, while others simply give up trying. Eventually they become dropouts when with a little extra help and prayer they could succeed. With a touch from God they can excel and live fulfilling lives. Scripture tells us to seek knowledge and with knowledge get understanding. But they need our prayers!

"God has put it on my heart to pray for my grandchildren and for other children struggling with their schoolwork. I've prayed for many and have seen remarkable answers right away. My granddaughter Marcy is my special darling because she loves me so much. Whenever she had a hard time in school, she would call me on the phone, 'Grandma, please pray. I have a test at a certain time and I need God's help.' She studied and I prayed. God always helped her.

"She went through grade school and high school with all A's, except for one B. She won many scholarships, graduated from the University of California, and went on to study for her master's degree. Her major is music, and she always has wanted to go to Europe, where many of the great composers were born.

"Recently, one of her friends whose father is a travel agent was able to get her a free ticket for three weeks in Europe. She is so excited she can hardly contain herself. She is a dedicated Christian and wants only God's will for her life. God has promised that if our ways please him, he will give us the desires of our heart" (see Ps. 37:4–5).

"You'll Make It . . . I'm Praying for You"

Carrie, a woman in her thirties, told us how her great-grandmother's prayers had encouraged her as a child. She remembered how Nana had always believed in her and told her that she could do well in school and succeed. Recalling those prayers, Carrie perservered long after Nana's death. Along the way, a few teachers and substitute grandmas cheered her on, even when she felt dumb. She writes, "I grew up thinking I was not smart, because I didn't learn like all the other kids. School was a pain for me. It took me five-and-a-half years to get a four-year college degree. But I'd remember Nana's prayers for me when she was alive. 'You'll make it, sugar baby,' she would say. 'You can conquer those studies; I'm praying for you.'

"In my late twenties I went through a series of learning tests, and the results showed me how I could learn more effectively. I am most thankful for the positive people who came into my life, people who said things such as:

"'You are *not* dumb. Silly, maybe, but not dumb.'
"'If you quit now, you'll set a pattern for the rest of your life.'
"'Don't be so hard on yourself.'
"'You *will* graduate!'

"God and others were responsible for the achievements in my life. My Nana always told me I could do things other people can't. I guess that's why I can enjoy my own particular style of 'fun art,' for it helps in my job as an illustrator for children's books."

No doubt thousands of children out there, like Carrie, think of themselves as dumb or inadequate in many areas. We who are older and wiser have a unique opportunity to be sensitive and available to talk when a grandchild is ready to open up, whether to share a failure or a victory, a happy moment or a disappointment. They need to hear from us, "Come on, you can do it! I'm praying for you. I believe in you."

As we've seen through the stories in this chapter, with prayer and support from a grandma or a substitute grandma, our grandchildren can be encouraged to keep going to achieve their goals. What a wonderful privilege and opportunity we grandmothers have!

Prayer

Lord, I pray for the protection of my grandchildren in the classroom, on the playground, on the school bus, in the carpool. Watch over their coming and going, and watch over them while they are on campus. Give them discernment and wisdom, and help them keep alert to danger. I pray for the right friends to come into their lives at the proper time. Give them godly, like-minded friends, and may they be a good influence on one another. Help my grandchilden to apply themselves well in their studies and to use the talents you have given them to their full potential. Lord, I pray their lives will always glorify you. In Jesus' name. Amen.

Helpful Scriptures

Get wisdom, get understanding;
    do not forget my words or swerve from them.
Do not forsake wisdom, and she will protect you;
    love her, and she will watch over you.

—Proverbs 4:5–6

"My command is this: Love each other as I have loved you. Greater love has no one than this, that he lay down his life for his friends. You are my friends if you do what I command."

—John 15:12–14

Don't let anyone look down on you because you are young, but set an example for the believers in speech, in life, in love, in faith and in purity.

—1 Timothy 4:12

Scripture Prayer

Father, I claim this promise for my grandchildren [names] while they are at school: that you will instruct them and teach them in the way they should go, that you will counsel them and watch over them [Ps. 32:8].

In every endeavor they undertake, all my grandchildren are more than conquerors through Christ who loves them [Rom. 8:37].

Related Scripture References

Proverbs 1; 13:20
Romans 12:9–13
1 Corinthians 5:9–11

Praying for Protection and Health

For he will command his angels concerning you
to guard you in all your ways;
they will lift you up in their hands,
so that you will not strike your foot against a stone.

—Psalm 91:11–12

*Prayer is sweeping my grandchildren into my arms when
they are afraid—thanking God with them for His protection. It is pacing with an infant granddaughter with colic,
breathing a continuous prayer for relief. It is including
God's comfort along with the bandage on a skinned knee.*

—Evelyn Christenson,
What Happens When We Pray for Our Families?

Every parent and grandparent is concerned about the safety and
protection of the children in their care, and of course we take normal precautions against danger. But what a comfort to know that
through our prayers, we can see God's hand of protection over
them when it's beyond our power to keep them safe.

Recently, I (Ruthanne) read a story in our local newspaper about a nine-year-old girl who had been kidnapped while playing outside her apartment complex one Sunday afternoon. A stranger approached and asked her to show him how to operate the machinery in the laundromat. When she went with him, he grabbed her, bound her wrists together, shoved her into his car, and sped off. A search began right away but turned up nothing. After three days, authorities held out little hope that she would be found alive.

On the fourth day, a reporter found a woman and her sister sitting on the steps near where the child had disappeared. "You see us sitting here?" the woman said. "I'm waiting to see my granddaughter walk up here. That's what I'm waiting for and praying for and hoping for. We're waiting for her to come home."[1]

Less than twenty-four hours later, that's exactly what happened. On Friday, the fifth day after her disappearance, at six-thirty in the morning, the child's abductor dropped her off about a block from her apartment. She ran across the complex, knocked on her parents' door, and was reunited with her family. While being held captive in a boarded-up cabin outside the city, she convinced the man who had kidnapped her to take her back home. You can imagine how that grandmother must have rejoiced, along with other members of the family, who agreed the miracle was in response to prayer.

Even the police chief said, "I really can't speak as to what was his [the captor's] thought process. . . . Personally, I fall back on my faith. And we had some divine intervention here."

When our grandchildren's safety is at stake, what is truly important in life comes into perspective. It's in times like these, when we're suddenly aware of how desperately we need divine help, that our faith in God is tested. The grandparents in our next story faced just such a test.

Praying for Their Safety

Grandmother Liz and her husband, James, enjoyed an outing with their two grandchildren to visit a tourist attraction in Orlando.

But before the day was over, they were crying out to God for the children's safety. "Little did we know what a terrifying experience lay ahead of us on that balmy Florida afternoon," Liz said.

After seeing several shows and exhibits, the grandparents decided to give Susie and Aaron, four-year-old cousins, some free time on the gigantic playground. Liz commented to James that there were hardly any children around and no crowds were nearby, so she felt it was okay to turn them loose for a while.

"Susie, who was quite a climber, immediately scaled a pole and quickly disappeared into a large plastic tunnel," Liz said. "As soon as she was out of sight, we noticed to our horror that a huge crowd began pouring out of a nearby stadium, and the once quiet play-ground was suddenly filled with hundreds of children and adults milling around. In an instant, Aaron also had wandered out of sight. We were in a sea of humanity and our grandchildren had been swallowed up. Vanished."

After a while they spied Aaron in his red sunsuit, and James managed to reach him in time to scoop him up in his arms. But no Susie. Hundreds of little faces, but no Susie. "I felt sick at my stomach as a wave of fear washed over me," Liz said. "So many young children had been kidnapped in public places. Only recently the newspaper had published a story about a young girl being raped and murdered not far from Orlando. 'Oh, James,' I cried, 'we must pray!' As I held onto little Aaron with one hand and grabbed James' hand with the other, we stood in a prayer circle in the midst of the crowd. We prayed for Susie's safe return, asking God to send angels to protect her."

"'I'm sure God will answer our prayer,' James said anxiously. 'Let's notify the park office and find out if they have a lost chil-dren's station somewhere.'"

They found a park attendant, but he was no help at all. He was new on the job and had no idea what should be done to try to find a lost child.

"God, I trust you, but I am so scared," Liz prayed desperately. "Please, please, let us find our baby girl before something bad hap-pens to her."

Prayers for Protection and Health

Here are some Scripture-based prayers you can pray for your grandchildren's protection and health:

Thank you, Lord, that I can proclaim this blessing over my grandchildren: The Lord will keep [names] from all harm; he will watch over their lives, the Lord will watch over their coming and going both now and forevermore [Ps. 121:7–8].

Thank you, Lord, that you are faithful to strengthen my grandchildren and protect them from the evil one [2 Thess. 3:3].

I pray that my grandchildren [names] may enjoy good health and that all may go well with them, even as their souls get along well [3 John 2].

I pray my grandchildren will acquire good health habits and not abuse their bodies, remembering that their bodies are "temples" where your Spirit lives and are therefore sacred [1 Cor. 3:16].

"Because [name] loves me," says the Lord, "I will rescue [name]; I will protect [him/her], for [name] acknowledges my name. [Name] will call upon me and I will answer [him/her]; I will be with [name] in trouble, I will deliver and honor [him/her]. With long life will I satisfy [him/her] and show [name] my salvation" [Ps. 91:14–16].

After giving a report to the park office, they decided to split up and cover the entire playground by walking back and forth. Still clutching Aaron's hand, Liz pulled him along and continued praying aloud for Susie as she walked and searched through the throng of people.

"Twenty minutes had passed, but it seemed like hours," she said. "Suddenly, I saw James coming toward me, smiling. But where was Susie? Then I saw her head just behind his; she was being held in the arms of the most beautiful teenage girl I'd ever seen. As they approached, James' smile widened into a big grin. 'This young lady found Susie!' he said jubilantly. 'Realizing that our girl was lost, she's been carrying Susie around all this time looking for us.'"

Tears of relief splashed down Liz's cheeks as she took Susie into her arms and hugged her close. "Thank you, God, oh, thank you!" she sobbed. When she turned to thank the young lady, she had already melted into the crowd. As far as Liz is concerned, she was an angel of protection.

Warning Voice: "Go Home"

Hazel and her husband, Gene, were shopping one Saturday when suddenly she was aware of an inner voice saying, *Go home.* She told Gene and he had had the same impression, so they rushed home. The phone was ringing as they walked in the house.

"It was our younger daughter calling to say our two-year-old grandson, Ray, had been run over and his mom was on the way to the hospital with him," Hazel said. "Then my daughter screamed, 'Ray isn't breathing, Mom! Pray!'"

The grandparents rushed to the hospital, praying in agreement that none of Ray's bones were broken and that God would let him live. "Lord, if I can't hear my little Ray call me 'Drama' again, I don't think I can live," Hazel cried.

At the hospital they got the details of the accident. Their son-in-law's brother, Archie, who lives next door to the family, had driven home with bags of cement in the back of his pickup. His children and little Ray had run out to greet him, but Archie decided to move the truck closer to the house to unload it. When he backed up, he ran over Ray, then without noticing what had just happened, he drove forward and ran over him again.

Realizing the horrible thing he'd just done, Archie jumped out of the truck and scooped up Ray's body, sobbing. The child's mother, Linda, tried to take him from Archie's arms, but the man was in shock and wouldn't let go of the baby. Linda shoved Archie in the car while he continued holding Ray, and drove as fast as she could for the hospital. It appeared that Ray never drew a breath until they pulled into the hospital parking lot. It had been a seven-mile drive and almost twenty minutes had elapsed. It was at this exact moment that the grandparents, Hazel and Gene, were alerted to pray.

"Believe me, we prayed all the way to the hospital," Hazel said. "When we finally got to see our grandson, the tire marks across his body were clearly visible. The pressure of the truck had caused some of the capillaries in his body to break, making measle-like blotches. Amazingly, the doctors found no broken bones. Ray limped for a few days but had no negative aftereffects. It was a miraculous answer to our prayers. God gave him back his life, and Ray grew up to be a fine young man."

Praying to Maintain Good Health

One grandmother we know says she prays often and specifically for her grandchildren to maintain good health, as their parents' religion doesn't believe in getting medical care for them when they are ill. She finds ways to share with her grandchildren her two special loves: teaching preschoolers in Sunday school, and volunteering at a hospital to serve patients and cheer them up. Whenever she has the opportunity, she tells her grandchildren exciting stories of Jesus' touching people's lives, both in Bible days and now, among the patients she serves. They listen with polite interest, and she's pleased that sometimes they ask questions about Jesus.

Jean is a praying grandmother who was halfway around the world on a tour when she got word that her two-year-old grandson, Josiah, was sick. He had been running a dangerously high fever for several days, and the doctors couldn't discover why. Late that night after getting the message, Jean, her husband, and some friends on the tour joined them in their hotel room to pray for Josiah's healing. After a persistent, intense time of prayer, Jean felt peace about the situation.

The next day, word came that Josiah's temperature had dropped, although doctors still were not sure why he'd become ill in the first place. Though Jean had at first been upset that she wasn't at home to pray for him in person, she found that long-distance praying will do. "God is always listening to the cries of our hearts, no matter where we are," she said. "This situation reminded me of that."

Life is full of disappointments, sorrows, and surprises, yet we must face them, depending on God to sustain us with his grace and wisdom. The grandmother in our next story learned the reality of God's faithfulness in the midst of years of heartache for her family.

Protection and Restoration

Trena was thrilled to become a grandmother when little Paul was born, yet from the beginning she was concerned about his safety and the environment he was growing up in.

"A month before she graduated from college, my daughter, Lisa, married Dan, a choice that greatly troubled me and my husband. Two years later, when our precious grandson, Paul, was born, we were worried because Dan didn't work, help with the baby, or do much of anything around the house.

"I owned an executive recruiting firm, and since Lisa had worked for me for several years, she knew the business very well. I turned it over to her, and she ran the operation out of her home so she could take care of the baby. Because she had good experience and business sense, Lisa began making a great deal of money, but she seemed to be changing from the loving daughter I had known. She was keeping company with a very fast crowd, and I became more and more concerned about the baby's safety. Later I learned it was during this time that Lisa started her downward spiral with drugs, something she had told me she would never do.

"I'd go to Lisa's house to keep Paul and find her in her office working, but Dan would still be in bed at one o'clock in the afternoon. If I tried to talk to her about Dan's not having a job, it made her angry. Then she started traveling on weekends—'On business,' she said. But I knew it would be highly unusual for her to be conducting executive recruiting business on weekends. I was concerned about little Paul and continually prayed for his protection.

"One week when I got home from an out-of-town trip, I found that Lisa had left Paul with Dan and had moved in with a friend. Our grandson was alone with this irresponsible man who had no job, had never spent much time with his son, and was known to be doing drugs! My husband and I were dumbfounded. How could Lisa be so careless?

"Finally, she admitted to having an affair and filed for divorce. She gave Dan custody of Paul except for every other weekend and one night during the week. Several months later, she came to live with us—broke, thousands of dollars in debt, and continually receiving calls from creditors. Still, there was no reasoning with her. We got her an office and I cashed in all my savings to try to help her reestablish the business, but it was impossible.

"Dan moved to his mother's house in a town nearby, taking the baby with him. Both our grandson's parents were doing drugs, and we felt helpless to know what to do about it. At one point, a major drug dealer began calling our home, threatening to kill Lisa and us if she didn't pay him what she owed. Because of horror stories we'd heard, we paid the money but later realized that was a mistake.

"One day in my Bible reading I came across this verse: 'the seed of the righteous shall be delivered' [Prov. 11:21 KJV]. I claimed that promise and began declaring it continually day and night, asking God to help me to do the right thing. As Lisa's situation unfolded, he began showing me that I was harboring hatred, a desire for revenge, and a tendency to try to manipulate and control people and situations. I humbled myself before the Lord, forgave my son-in-law and my daughter, and asked God to cleanse my heart.

"I began to claim and confess these promises daily [based on Prov. 11:21 and Isa. 54:13 KJV]: 'The seed of the righteous shall be delivered.' 'My child and grandchild will be taught by the Lord and great shall be their peace.'

"I found Scriptures pertaining to salvation for my loved ones and quoted them out loud continually. I was persistent—asking, seeking, knocking, while giving thanks to God.

"One after another, miracles started happening! I placed Lisa in a rehabilitation center, for she was now pregnant. She and Dan were divorced and he still had Paul. I realized Dan's parents were condoning Lisa's lifestyle because it meant they could keep the baby. When they refused to let me see my grandson, I filed suit for grandparents' visitation rights.

"In our state, if a grandparent has contributed financially to the care of a grandchild and has spent a great deal of time with that child, the court can award him or her visitation rights or custody. Thank God I had kept receipts for all the things I had bought for Paul over the past two years, plus his medical bills and some of his day-care bills. When we went to court, I had witnesses and receipts. I also let the judge know that I had put Lisa in rehab and that she was six months pregnant.

"The judge awarded me grandparents' visitation rights two weekends a month. Because Lisa had expressed such hatred toward me at the hearings, he ordered us to go for joint counseling for six months. It was a struggle, but through much prayer, our relationship was healed. She finally realized that Dan and his parents were against her and that her own parents actually were trying to help her.

"As soon as I realized Lisa had been using cocaine from the time she had conceived her second child, I began praying for the baby. I asked God to protect this child in the womb and let him or her be born physically whole, with a clear mind and no addictions. When Lisa got out of rehab, we helped her buy a house, and she slowly began thinking rationally and clearly. She regained custody of Paul, and God has totally restored the bond between us— no mother and daughter get along better than we do. I believe she has renewed her commitment to the Lord, and she's becoming more comfortable with going back to church.

"Shannon, our beautiful granddaughter, was born perfectly normal—truly a miracle baby. God answered every prayer I had prayed for her! When Lisa resumed working, I kept Shannon for the first year and a half. She is now almost three and thriving in a Christian day care, and Paul is in preschool. I take the children to church on Sunday, and they spend at least one night a week with me. It's a joy and a privilege for me to baby-sit my grandchildren and pray over them.

"Lisa loves both her children, and now, at last, she's becoming the mother God intended her to be. She is now married to Andrew, a man with many excellent qualities. But the main thing is, he loves my daughter and grandchildren, and all three of them love and respect him. How blessed I am to see a walking miracle every day when I look at Lisa, Andrew, Paul, and Shannon. Not only did God reach down and snatch Lisa out of the pit, he gave us these two precious grandchildren, and soon we will have a third."

When we go through an ordeal as terrifying as Trena's, it's easy to give in to worrying about those we're praying for and sometimes to be really angry with them. God can help us overcome these obstacles and see our prayers answered, but first our attitudes must change.

"In my desperation, as well as my exasperation with my faith in God, I was tormented by worry at one point," Trena said. "The ironic thing was I knew it, yet I couldn't seem to rise above it. Finally I found myself pouring my heart out to some friends who listened and prayed for me, my daughter, and my grandchildren. God had prepared the people and the way for his Word to be fulfilled in my life."

A Special Grandchild

What's a mother to do when she learns her twenty-eight-year-old son—her pride and joy—got his girlfriend pregnant? This was the quandary facing a woman we'll call Mariah, who felt the girl, Erin, was bent on marrying her son, Forrest. Though she invited the couple over for family dinners a few times, they still didn't get very well acquainted.

Then the baby was born. At four pounds she was not only a

preemie, but she had multiple medical problems. Doctors had her airlifted to a nearby medical center, where they immediately operated to correctly align her esophagus. Among other problems, she had no bladder, her only kidney was only 60 percent functional, and the growth bone in her left arm was missing and she had a tiny twisted hand at the end. This condition, Bader Syndrome, occurs because of a missing gene that prevents organs and bones from forming normally. So here was little Karen with a series of physical defects, weighing only four pounds.

When the doctor advised Forrest to let them take her off life support, he came out of the room and collapsed with sobs. The grandparents called intercessors all over the United States for prayer. People took up prayer vigils in the lobby and hall of the hospital, hour after hour.

Grandmother Mariah remembers the heartbreaking dilemma. Was it better for this baby to die and go on to heaven? Or should they pray in faith, believing she had a greater chance to live than the doctors were predicting? The most optimistic prognosis was that she would constantly have to wear a urine bag and her maimed arm could not be repaired.

Her dad decided early on that he would fight for this child's life, though he had no insurance. A year after the birth, her parents married.

Little Karen underwent surgery after surgery. For the first three years of her life, she was on life-support machines from time to time, even at home. Someone had to stay with her night and day. She couldn't go through all the normal crawling, standing, and walking stages most children do.

Once when she was two and a half and in the hospital with another life-threatening situation—scar tissue from a surgery was causing her to vomit up everything—I (Quin) stood over her small form and prayed for her to live. Mariah and I had been friends for years, and when I was in her city to speak for a retreat, she asked me to visit the hospital and pray for Karen. I wanted to offer my prayer support for my friend's grandchild, yet I knew it would take a miracle of God to save her.

Today Karen is eight years old and in the second grade at a Christian school, but her medical problems continue. Her immune system is fragile, so when any germs or bacteria attack her body, she goes back to the hospital, facing another crisis. But she has such a happy spirit, such a will to live, she is an inspiration to anyone who meets her.

Karen and her grandmother Mariah are close buddies. Mariah has taught her how to be sensitive to the voice of the Lord and how to memorize Scripture. When she was just learning to talk, she'd say, "One God, come down to love his people." Then she'd wrap her arms about herself, showing how much God loves her.

She has big, brown eyes, soft brown hair, and never meets a stranger because of all the "strangers" she's been around during her hospital stays. Recently in her grandmother's Sunday school class, she stood up to introduce herself. "Well, I have a little crooked hand, but I can really read good. And I love Jesus." The class applauded.

One afternoon when Karen's urine bag leaked and she got wet, she was embarrassed and cold and discouraged. Grandmother Mariah picked her up from school and took her home with her to clean her up. Then the two of them crawled into bed to keep warm and had a grandmother-granddaughter chat.

"Karen, you got outside your comfort zone today and became fearful and embarrassed," Mariah told her. "But you know, that's where God is, too. He's there to help you through these situations. Just tell him how you feel, and don't let anyone make you feel embarrassed when something happens that is out of your control."

"Okay, Nana," she said. That night she couldn't wait to tell her younger brother about how God is with us even when we step out of our comfort zones. Grandmother Mariah and Granddad John have showered her with "you are special" items, making her feel accepted and loved. Mariah holds tightly to the Scripture, "Behold, I and the children whom the LORD has given me are for signs and wonders" (Isa. 8:18 NASB). She believes Karen is for signs and wonders, and every day she lives is another sign of God's mercy.

Another breakthrough in this family is that Mariah and her daughter-in-law, Erin, now have a close relationship. Erin even occasionally attends a Bible study class with her mother-in-law.

"This little family lives at crisis-management level every day," Mariah said. "They aren't yet overcomers, but I truly expect them all to be someday. It's not wishful thinking. God is a rewarder of those who diligently seek him."

Grandmother Mariah now faces a heart-pulling challenge, to let go as Forrest plans to move his family to another town an hour away to shorten his commute. Karen will have to switch schools, and grandmother and granddaughter won't have so much time together. But Mariah has six other grandchildren to keep up with through letters and phone calls and visits. And she trusts God to help Karen to grow stronger and keep overcoming every medical obstacle she faces. She's a spunky girl who knows her God!

In her book *What Is a Family?* Edith Schaeffer reminds us that the phrase "in sickness and in health" in the wedding vow applies to the whole family. Times of injury or sickness will visit every household at one time or another, but, she writes, "a family should be a place where comfort is experienced and understood, so that the people are prepared to give comfort to others. Comfort should be related to the word *family*. . . . God can use us *because* of the difficulty, sickness, handicap, tragedy—not in *spite* of it—to do something which He has for us to do, and which we otherwise could not have done."[2]

When life's crises do occur, we grandmothers can be a steadying force through prayer and encouragement to help stabilize our families.

Prayer

Lord, I ask for your divine protection over my grandchildren. Thank you that you are their healer and can touch their bodies when they are ill or injured. Lord, please keep them alert so they won't be lured into perilous situations, and prompt me to pray when they're in any kind of danger. I give you thanks for all the ways you have intervened in their lives so far in protecting them and restoring their health. Amen.

Helpful Scriptures

God is our refuge and strength,
an ever-present help in trouble.
—Psalm 46:1

The LORD will keep you from all harm—
he will watch over your life;
the LORD will watch over your coming and going
both now and forevermore.
—Psalm 121:7–8

I am the LORD, who heals you.
—Exodus 15:26

I pray that you may enjoy good health and that all may go well with you, even as your soul is getting along well.
—3 John 2

People brought to [Jesus] all who were ill with various diseases, those suffering severe pain, the demon-possessed, those having seizures, and the paralyzed, and he healed them.
—Matthew 4:24

Scripture Prayer

Lord, I pray for each one of my grandchildren [names] that they will lie down and sleep in peace, for you alone, O LORD, make them dwell in safety [Ps. 4:8]. Lord, please turn to my grandchild [name] and be gracious to [him/her], for [he/she] is lonely and the troubles of [his/her] heart have multiplied. Look upon [him/her] in [his/her] distress and move by your mighty power to heal [him/her] [Ps. 25:16–18].

Related Scripture References

Deuteronomy 31:6; 33:26–27
Psalms 23; 91; 121
Isaiah 26:3–4
Matthew 28:20

Praying for Hurting Grandchildren

Praise be to the God and Father of our Lord Jesus Christ, the Father of compassion and the God of all comfort, who comforts us in all our troubles, so that we can comfort those in any trouble with the comfort we ourselves have received from God.

—2 Corinthians 1:3–4

We turn to Grandmother trusting that she will help us find answers, show us beauty and wonder, and call us to full personhood. She not only knows what we do not know; she also is wise enough to take time with us until we learn it. No other woman can make a child feel so handsome, so clever, so skillful, so loved, as a grandmother.

—Kristen Johnson Ingram,
I'll Ask My Grandmother—She's Very Wise

How hard it is to watch our grandchildren struggle with their hurts, whether emotional or physical illnesses, disabilities, or disappointment and rejection. A child with leukemia fighting for her life. An adopted grandchild coming to terms with feelings of abandonment.

A child with a poor self-image who feels overshadowed by the talent of a gifted sibling. Another who seems consumed by rage.

No matter what the circumstances, prayer can work wonders, bringing peace in a situation of great confusion, and hope where there is desperation. Too often we waste our energy fretting and worrying about our grandchildren when they face crises. But our time and strength can be spent in a more productive way by seeking God for his direction and by determining how to pray on target.

Facing the Lion's Den

Janet's story is an example of how a godly grandmother can have a powerful influence on a grandchild living in a dreadful home situation.

"During the very early years of Daniel's life, I tucked him in bed every night while his mother, my daughter, worked as a nurse in a nearby hospital," she wrote. "I read him Bible stories—his favorite, of course, was Daniel and the Lion's Den—and then we prayed together, asking for God's protection while we slept. Little did I know then that facing a roaring lion every day of his life would be his greatest challenge."

When Daniel was four years old, his mother married a man who, from all appearances, seemed as though he would be a good father to Janet's grandson. But this was not the case. Rather, it was the beginning of a long nightmare for the young boy. The situation could have destroyed his self-esteem and motivation, except for prayer and encouragement from his mother and grandmother.

"The verbal abuse he suffered continuously was horrendous; I'm certain it was only God's hand on him and the many prayers of all who loved him that helped him survive," Janet said. "My daughter did not believe in divorce, but her witness and love and prayer support sustained my grandson. Daniel's mom was not only his homeschool teacher, she also coached him in memorizing Scripture. He was on the church's Bible quiz team and helped them win many competitions. This is a perfect example of how

God's Word, written on a young person's heart, can protect him and cause him to thrive even through adversity."

Each year, Daniel grew stronger in his faith, and as a teenager he shared his faith with others as a member of a youth ministry team. Still the verbal and emotional abuse by his stepfather continued, with Daniel being made the scapegoat for anything that went wrong at home. At one point Grandma Janet enlisted her Bible study group to join her in praying for him.

"God has answered my prayers by delivering him from that hurtful situation," she said. "Daniel is now seventeen years old and living with me. I know God has special plans for him. I continue to pray that he will direct Daniel's career choices now that he's starting college and use him mightily for his purposes. How thankful I am that we serve a God who can take what's wrong and make it right! I'm believing God for Daniel's stepfather's salvation, knowing that no one is out of his reach."

Sylvia is a praying grandmother who teaches in a primary public school because it gives her an opportunity to help hurting children. Besides praying for her grandkids, she prays for her young pupils as if they were her grandchildren.

"I believe that children are God's greatest gift to us, yet they are the most neglected in our society," she said. "Recently, in a single day, three of my public school second-graders asked me to pray for them because of serious problems in their homes. After I prayed, I encouraged them to pray for one another. Then I suggested to these seven-year-olds that when their parents start arguing, they can find a quiet spot by themselves and talk to God. I'm glad I can be here for these hurting kids who probably don't have a praying grandmother."

Faith to Fight Giants

Catherine has always taught her children the vital importance of prayer, and so when her daughter, Freda, wanted a family, they prayed. Her first pregnancy ended in miscarriage, and in the second, she had serious problems that required an immediate C-section before the baby was full term. Little Miriam weighed only four pounds, but all of her internal organs were fully developed, and at three weeks, she was discharged from the hospital weighing five pounds.

"This was a blessing, since most preemies aren't dismissed until they weigh more," Grandmother Catherine said. "But doctors allowed Miriam to go home because she seemed so healthy."

The child had no more health problems until one fall day when she was seven. After a month of her not feeling well, doctors determined Miriam had hepatitis C, then ordered an intestinal sonogram. When the technician made an extra high swoop across her tummy, she noticed the tip of Miriam's heart.

"This caused much alarm because a petite seven-year-old should not have such an enlarged heart," Grandmother Catherine said. "When the doctor hospitalized her for more tests, they discovered she had severe cardiac problems and immediately flew her to a children's hospital in a nearby city. Many intercessors joined our family in praying for Miriam's life."

For three uncertain weeks, doctors discussed the possibility of heart replacement surgery, then finally decided against it. But through it all, the family experienced a sense of God's peace. With each new challenge, they seemed to receive another measure of supernatural strength as they took turns staying with Miriam in the hospital. After four weeks, doctors said if she could take her heart medications orally without negative reactions, she would be able to return home for a while.

Catherine stayed with the youngster during this period so her parents could go home to catch up on affairs. The first night after she began taking oral medications, Miriam did fine. However, the next morning after breakfast, she became nauseated. She was upset because both her parents were going to be gone for two days, and the anxiety was affecting her stomach.

Grandmother Catherine began telling Miriam the Bible story about the shepherd boy David and the giant Goliath, who wanted to destroy the people of Israel. David defeated the giant with only a slingshot because God was with him and had prepared him to fight this battle.

"Has God ever done anything like that for you?" Catherine asked the girl. "Has he ever rewarded your faith by giving you the desires of your heart?"

Miriam's eyes lit up as she told her grandmother how she had prayed she would be able to keep Mazey, her pet kitten. God had changed her mom's heart so she didn't have to give the cat away. Then Catherine reminded Miriam of the time when she had been living with her grandparents and she'd asked God to give her her very own bedroom. It wasn't long before her folks were able to buy a house and she had her own special room. As they reminisced about God's faithfulness, Miriam's nausea faded and she became peaceful.

"I reminded her that her daddy was helping her learn Bible verses so she could be strong like David," Catherine said, "and that all of us in the family are praying for her, but that she, too, could stand up against the giants in her life. Miriam is back at home now, still taking medications but waiting in faith for her miracle. She is strong, like David, worshiping God with all her heart and declaring defeat to her sickness."

One day as Catherine was driving to the hospital, she felt that God spoke to her through this verse: "The word of the LORD came to me, saying, 'Before I formed you in the womb I knew you, before you were born I set you apart'" (Jer. 1:5).

"While we wait in faith for God to heal Miriam's heart, I take comfort in the fact that God formed her in the womb, knew her, and set her apart for his purposes," Catherine said.

Praying for Grandchildren with Special Problems

When a grandchild suffers with a disability or genetic disease, a grandparent usually is face to face with her own hurt and disappointment. In learning to cope, she must allow God to readjust her attitude and help her to look at the situation differently. From Nancy's journal entries, written over a two-year period, we get a glimpse of a grandmother's heart when she learns that her grandchild was born with a disability.

"Our grandson, Jacob, was born today with possible Down's syndrome. At first I felt like the wind was knocked out of me. Unreality. Denial. Hope. Reality. Peace. This world has no guarantees. God's plan and purpose is standing, despite what feels like a mistake. Our support has come from praying friends.

"I've discovered as the days have passed that I have a very shallow measuring rod. God is so much bigger and wiser. I've faced my prejudice about retarded people more closely. God sees them as people of worth. I tend to measure everyone by his or her contribution to society and family, or by beauty, education, talent. I have been relearning and changing how I view people, seeing them from God's perspective, not through my tainted and fallen and perverse one. The Holy Spirit has been faithful to help me, of course.

"I baby-sat for two-month-old Jacob today, and something very special happened when he woke up from his nap. I went in to pick him up, and he smiled at me. I fed him his bottle, and he cooed and smiled again. It's like a down payment on more to come! Yesterday a couple in California wrote of their granddaughter with Down's. So encouraging, as they said every gift God gives is a good one and that we've been given a very special blessing from the Lord. I could only receive a word like that from someone who's been there. This is a completely new path for all of us. I'm glad he's in charge and that we can lean on the Lord.

"Jacob seems to take delight in all of life—to squeeze more out of it than the average child. He laughs, kisses, hugs, and claps so often. He loves learning new things and repeating them over and over. He is learning sign language to minimize the frustration of delayed speech. His colostomy reversal was in August, and he's fully recovered. Some people are repulsed by him; others are tender and compassionate."

Nancy's prayer: "Thank you, Lord, for this chance to trust you when I cannot understand it all. Help me to keep my eyes on Jesus and his eternal, long-range view. He has the telescope. He loves us—me, Jacob—just because we're people made to reflect his glory. Jacob and people like him offer us a chance to be compassionate and loving, not mean, narrow, and bigoted. This is a faith crisis for me. I am trusting you, my Father, to do what's best. Accomplish your perfect will for all involved. May Jacob come to know you at an early age and always love and praise you. Let him go beyond the limits the doctors set for him, to accomplish your will and purpose for his life. I trust you to do this, my Savior. Amen."

Praying for a Grandson's Disability

Susan and her husband, whose eighteen-year-old grandson, Jerry, has muscular dystrophy, recently moved from another state to be closer to him. They pray, laugh, and talk together about anything on Jerry's heart and study Scriptures on healing and heaven. He's already lived longer than doctors expected he would, and they want as much time with him as possible.

"I keep asking the Lord to heal Jerry and give him a long, productive life," Susan said. "I pray for his parents to have strength, peace, and courage in caring for him at home. I praise God for allowing this child to be in my life for however long it may be and for all the joy he brings to our family. I pray for God to lead the hands and direct the minds of the doctors and all associated with my grandson's treatment. I also pray for medical breakthroughs for this disease."

Here is one grandmother's prayer for a child with minor difficulties: "Lord, my prematurely born grandchild, who has suffered a speech impediment and other problems all his life, is now leaving for school in a city far away from his family. I'm concerned because he still stutters and is slower than others. He'll be in classes with bright, active students. Lord, help him keep up with his schoolwork. Give him a sense of purpose as he studies in his field of interest. Give his instructors compassionate hearts as they teach and encourage him. Thank you, Lord, for loving him, guiding him, and protecting him as he will now live on his own. Continue to touch his body with your healing power, and help him to cope with his limitations. Amen."

A grandmother whose grandchild is autistic prays, "Lord, my grandchild is autistic and her parents have placed her in a home with others like her, though it's two hours from their house. I've agonized over this decision. Yet it was theirs to make. She'd grown too rough for her mother to handle—physically strong and destructive to herself and her surroundings. Now I pray that all who will be caring for this special child will have your wisdom. I pray for her protection and safety. Lord, may you somehow penetrate to her inner soul and let her know she is loved and accepted. Amen."

Grandparents' Prayers Prevail

Pauline was living near me (Quin) in northwest Florida when she got a phone call that a new grandaughter, Toni, had been born in Mobile, Alabama. However, the news was not all good. The baby was having seizures, and a CT scan showed bleeding in the right front lobe of her brain.

As Pauline and her husband, Joe, jumped in the car to drive the 120 miles to the hospital, Joe prayed, "Lord, put a new artery in her brain. This child is flesh of my flesh, bone of my bone. Please, Lord, replace that bleeding artery. Thank you for hearing me."

After the two had prayed for about forty minutes, Joe felt a peace come over him. "I believe it's done," he said to Pauline. "I feel God's peace in this situation."

As soon as they reached the hospital, the neurosurgeon talked to both of them. Because he knew Pauline from her previous experience as a nurse, he said to her, "Now you know what this means; she will be paralyzed on the left side. You will have to arrange for lifetime care for her."

"I understand what you're saying," Pauline told the doctor. "*But God!* Our God is able to heal." Joe nodded in agreement and repeated, "But God . . ."

Toni's seizures stopped. The doctors showed the family the bleeding on the CT scans to prove what they had said was backed up medically. "But God . . ." the grandparents would repeat.

Pauline bought some Christian lullabies and a tape recorder with the request that the nurses play these songs in Toni's little isolette, which they did. Two days later, Toni was dismissed from the hospital. Because the doctors were sure of their diagnosis, they ran tests on her frequently for six months. But she never had another seizure.

Today Toni is twelve years old and in excellent health. Pauline and Joe are convinced the victory was won that day while they prayed in agreement on the way to the hospital. "I believe that at the moment Joe felt a release in his spirit, our grandbaby received a healing touch from God," she said.

Since they have seven children and twenty grandchildren, Pauline and Joe have a prayer notebook divided into seven sections. On each day of the week, they pray specifically for one child and his or her spouse and children that day. Of course, they pray for crises in their family as they arise, and they cover all the other children and grandchildren in a general prayer every day.

A Grandmother's Prayer Assignment

Bea felt God was giving her a new prayer assignment when her daughter, Corrie, and her husband got legal guardianship of their three-year-old nephew, Jed. Although Corrie had other children, Bea accepted Jed into the family as a grandson. She prayed for him regularly, just as she did for her other four grandchildren. Because his life had been so unstable due to his mother's drug addiction, she especially prayed for God to give him peace.

Jed was sometimes a troublesome child who struggled to fit in and often fretted because he couldn't live with his mom. As the years passed, he grew to hate what drugs had done to her, yet he was compassionate and very protective of his dysfunctional mother. His goal was to grow up, make a good living, and someday take care of her. At age nine, Jed accepted Jesus as his Savior, and he went to church regularly with the family.

One cold winter day soon after he'd turned eleven, he and his foster parents and older cousin had had a wonderful family day, playing board games and doing crafts. That evening everyone in the household went to bed early except Corrie, who stayed up to knit. Later, when she went to kiss Jed goodnight at around ten o'clock, she screamed for her husband to come quickly.

She had found Jed's lifeless body hanging from the top bunk bed with a belt around his neck. He'd been playing with the belt earlier that day, using it as a leash for his imaginary puppy. But somehow he'd gotten tangled up and evidently was trying to get undone when he pulled the belt the wrong way. Now an accident had claimed his life.

When Grandmother Bea got the phone call, she instantly began praying aloud, asking God to pour out his love on Corrie and her family. It was as if Bea's habit of praying for Jed had prepared the way for her passionate prayers when this tragedy occurred.

"I knew Jed was in heaven; I'd talked to him about his relationship with Jesus and was assured of that," she said. "But I also knew there was nothing Corrie and her husband could do to bring him back. I prayed that the entire family would receive God's comfort and peace without having to deal with false guilt or regret. They had given him a loving home and done everything for him that they'd done for their older son. Everyone knew it was an accident, and that helped them get over the tremendous loss. But only Jesus can bring comfort through something this traumatic."

Abused or Neglected Grandchildren

Author and psychologist Dr. John Trent speaks of grandparents as being God's "special agents" in giving love and acceptance to children who suffer from a lack of love and can easily grow up feeling worthless. He shares this vignette about a little girl, the youngest of six children, whose siblings made fun of her and told the neighbors she really wasn't their sister.

> Her grandparents lived just a few houses down as Judy was growing up. Her grandfather was a retired carpenter with bright, blue eyes and strong, gentle arms that hugged her every day. And her grandmother had the best lap to sit on for miles around.

Every day after school, she would run to her grandparents' home for a cookie or snack before heading home to the ridicule . . . and she wasn't just looking for something for her stomach. She was filling up her heart and soul before she headed into "the desert."

A little flour and sugar might make a good cookie, but even better were the words and actions that came warm and fresh from her grandparents. To them, she was always special, deeply loved, and greatly valuable. They, not her parents, took Judy to church and gave her a promise ring. They held out hope for a positive future for her. She devoured their "cookies for the heart" and now gives them freely to her own children and others. . . . When her parents were too busy to listen, Gramma and Grandpa had nothing but time.[1]

Here's a prayer for a grandchild suffering any form of neglect or abuse:

> *Lord, heal the emotional wounds my grandchild [name] has suffered because of rejection, ridicule, or physical or sexual abuse. Help me to reach out in love to offer comfort and a listening ear. Send friends and teachers across [his/her] path who can build [his/her] self-esteem and cause [him/her] to see [he/she] is valuable to you. Bring restoration by replacing the negative memories with a sense of security in your love. Keep [him/her] safe in body, soul, and spirit, Lord. I pray in Jesus' name. Amen.*

A Vicious Attack

Grandma Portia and her husband happened to be visiting their hometown when one of their grandchildren had a horrifying experience. Eight-year-old Sandy was walking home from a friend's house when two fierce dogs attacked her. A mother with a baby in a stroller had beaten the dogs off with her umbrella, causing them to run after Sandy. Neighbors watched helplessly as these ferocious animals kept biting the child. After an ambulance rushed Sandy to the hospital, someone called the grandparents.

As soon as Grandma Portia heard about the terrifying episode, she phoned several prayer partners in the area. They in turn alerted others to pray for the child. Sandy's mother worked for a team of doctors, and many of them rallied immediately to repair the severe damage done to the little girl's arm and leg. The skin on her right arm was peeled back, and the calf of her left leg was deeply cut by the bites.

"I was especially disturbed by this attack because I knew my young granddaughter had the same calling and anointing on her life for intercession that God had given me," Portia said. "I began to pray, 'Lord, I trust you, now. Come with your healing and help my granddaughter.' Then, addressing the enemy of my soul, I said aloud, 'In the name and by the authority of Jesus Christ of Nazareth, I declare the enemy's plan to disfigure my granddaughter—to put her in fear or to keep her in pain—is destroyed!'"

Since little Sandy lost much of her calf on one leg, she had to undergo several surgeries over the next year. Today at age fourteen, she is not disfigured, and the scars are barely noticeable. Remarkably, and no doubt due to her grandmother's continued prayers against fear, Sandy can be around dogs without fear of being bitten. Best of all, Sandy is enthusiastic about the Lord, Portia says, and is following in her grandmother's footsteps as an intercessor.

Encouraging Your Grandchild

All grandchildren need encouragement—someone to come alongside to offer comfort, praise, and reinforcement during every phase of their lives—especially when they're going through tough times. They need a person to tell them how much they are appreciated, accepted, and loved. They need cheerleaders. They need to hear, "You're going to make it! I'm here if you need to talk." What better person than a grandparent?

In addition to praying faithfully for your grandchildren, look for opportunities to encourage them with these day-brighteners. Add other attributes you can acknowledge in your grandchild. They need to know that you're an encourager and that you don't take them for granted. How many things can you tell your grandchildren you appreciate about them if you stop to name them right now? How many words of praise are on the tip of your tongue? Here are a few for starters:

"I'm really glad you're my grandchild."
"You are a neat guy."
"You're my little princess."
"You are so much fun."
"I'm so proud of you!"
"You are really a treasure."
"You make me laugh."
"You made my day."
"You're a good listener."
"You did a good job on that project."
"You obey your parents so well."
"Thank you for sharing with your sister [or brother]."
"You are a good friend."
"You were so kind to that little boy [or girl, lady, or man]."
"You really were brave in the dentist's [or doctor's] office."

Grandmothers Praying Together

As most of us probably have experienced, we grandmothers hurt, too, when our grandchildren are struggling through emotional or physical problems. And who better than another grandmother can relate to those feelings? Forming a partnership with another grandmother—or a group of two, three, or four—is a wonderful way to share problems, resources, and lessons learned. When one sees her prayers answered, it encourages the others to remain steadfast in faith while sharing the joy of their friend's victory.

Keep in mind, there is no distance in prayer! Our intercession for grandchildren transcends all time zones—all cultural, generational, and language barriers—as well as the limitations of our understanding. Praying with a prayer partner or a group helps keep this truth in perspective.

Pam and Jane have prayed together for more than twenty years—first for their daughters, now for their grandchildren. Since the one-time neighbors no longer live near one another, they frequently pray by phone. Pam says as soon as they learn one of their daughters is pregnant, they begin praying for the unborn child, claiming Christ's redemptive work on the cross for the expected grandchild.

"God promised to bless Abraham's seed, and there are many blessings promised in the Bible for the seed of the righteous," Pam said. "So we pray some of these promises for our grandchildren while they're still in the womb" (see Prov. 11:21 KJV).

One particular Scripture they pray is Isaiah 59:21: "'As for me, this is my covenant with them,' says the LORD. 'My Spirit, who is on you, and my words that I have put in your mouth will not depart from your mouth, or from the mouths of your children, or from the mouths of their descendants from this time on and forever,' says the LORD."

"We pray the Word, for we know we cannot go wrong with it," Pam says. "Great breakthroughs in our children's and grandchildren's lives have come through prayer."

Carmen and her walking partner, Sylvia, pray together as they walk around a school track early every morning. At least once a week they pray for their seventeen grandchildren, naming each one individually.

"It is a private outdoor prayer meeting," Carmen says. "Each of us prays however we feel the Holy Spirit leads as we share needs with one another, but we are committed to confidentiality. We have seen some wonderful answers to prayer: a child improving in school, another recovering quickly from an illness, and another working through a difficult stage. More than once, after prayer, we suggested to a parent that she take a child to the doctor when there was little visible reason to do it. But many ear infections were uncovered in this way."

The Benefit of Support Groups

Vivian feels one of the greatest benefits she's experienced in her family is belonging to the Christian support group she's been involved with for twenty-three years.

"I wonder whether I'd be a praying grandmother today if I hadn't been in this group," she said. "Our six children grew up with praying women in our home every Friday morning and thought it was normal Christian living; they were being mentored without realizing it. Today all of them belong to a home group of some kind, learning to love and pray for each other and for one another's children. Makes this praying grandmother's job much easier!"

Vivian's six children and seventeen grandchildren are widely scattered, but they communicate via telephone and e-mail daily and have family gatherings throughout the year. Her kitchen cabinets are covered with photos of her children and their families, and a framed photo of each grandchild hangs on the living room wall.

"I declare God's Word and pray blessings over each one of them every day," Vivian said. "Sometimes I find myself singing over them as the Lord directs me to a particular one that day. This prayer time is precious to me. When our children call for prayer needs, we pray together on the phone for the grandchildren, then later, my husband and I pray in agreement. The sweetest fruit is to pray with my husband and to see our grandchildren being raised by praying parents. Three of our oldest grandchildren are now in their own small home groups. Passing on to our children and grandchildren a rich spiritual heritage in Jesus is the greatest inheritance they can receive. It will flow through our family for generations to come."

Our Opportunity

We are often one step removed from the full responsibility and privilege of our grandchildren's daily care. This sometimes leaves us feeling unable to help or influence as much as we'd like when the children are hurting, especially if they are living with brokenness in their homes.

As shown in the stories of grandmothers in this chapter, we can find ways to be participants by offering our grandchildren encouragement, helping them find answers to perplexing questions, and making sure they feel loved, no matter what situation they're in.

But praying for our hurting precious ones is something we can do continually behind the scenes. God has placed us in their lives as prayer warriors for just such times as these. Our opportunity to pray is not a passive, idle way to pass the time when we can't "do" something. It is a mighty and powerful force we are invited to unleash. It is our opportunity for action!

Prayer

Lord, bring my grandchildren through their hurts to victory in you. May they trust you to heal rejection and disappointments, abandonment and jealousy, or whatever else troubles them. Please remove the pain of unpleasant memories, and give them joy and hope instead. Give me creative ways to respond to and comfort them in their times of hurt. Amen.

Helpful Scriptures

For the LORD comforts his people and will have compassion on his afflicted ones.

—Isaiah 49:13

"Peace I leave with you; my peace I give you. I do not give to you as the world gives. Do not let your hearts be troubled and do not be afraid."

—John 14:27

May our Lord Jesus Christ himself and God our Father, who loved us and by his grace gave us eternal encouragement and good hope, encourage your hearts and strengthen you in every good deed and word.

—2 Thessalonians 2:16–17

Scripture Prayer

Thank you, Lord, for being our refuge and strength, an ever present help in time of trouble. Lord, teach my grandchild [name] not to fear, no matter what happens, but to look to you, the maker of heaven and earth, for [his/her] help. Thank you for keeping [name] from harm and watching over [his/her] life [Pss. 46:1–2; 121:2, 7].

Related Scripture References

Psalms 23; 103
Isaiah 53
Romans 8:28–39

chapter 7

Praying for Families Broken by Death or Divorce

Let us hold firmly to the faith we profess. For we do not have a high priest who is unable to sympathize with our weaknesses, but we have one who has been tempted in every way, just as we are—yet was without sin. Let us then approach the throne of grace with confidence, so that we may receive mercy and find grace to help us in our time of need.

—Hebrews 4:14–16

It's so easy to focus on the negative characteristics in others. Instead, we need to see them as God sees them.... Look for the strengths and undeveloped potential in your family members. Your belief in them could be the catalyst which helps their hidden gifts to unfold. Your calling in difficult family relationships is not to contribute to the problem, but to contribute to the solution.

—H. Norman Wright, *Family Is Still a Great Idea*

Divorce or a death in the family causes anguish for our grandchildren, and for parents and grandparents as well. One grandmother experienced the heartache of having two beloved grandchildren ripped from her by divorce when the mother took the children and moved to a distant state. She wrote, "The pain of their leaving lived in the nooks and crannies of my heart until I decided to allow the Holy Spirit to take it away and replace it with hope. In the following weeks, God in His mercy showed me, day by day, that He was in control of the circumstances and that He would take care of me and those I love so dearly. I began to heal and learn that goodbye doesn't necessarily mean forever."[1]

Sometimes there is a window of opportunity to pray for the reconciliation of the parents, but that depends on the will of those involved. For the purpose of this book, our main prayer focus is the welfare of our grandchildren. When parents divorce, the children may suffer various consequences, such as:

- fear of the future
- feelings of rejection and loneliness
- alienation from God
- jealousy of friends whose parents are together
- financial hardship
- guilt that they somehow contributed to the divorce
- frustration in their relationship with the separated parents and/or their new partners
- unfocused anger that they themselves don't understand
- the complexities and challenges of building new relationships within blended families if one or both parents remarry

Grandparents—especially if they live nearby—can be a sounding board and a stabilizing force in the children's environment until their lives regain some normalcy. Allow your grandchildren to talk about their feelings and express their frustrations if they wish. But if they don't, just be there for them, offering unconditional love and hugs. And always let them know they're in your prayers.

Staying Connected Despite a Divorce

Maria was saddened when her family was torn by divorce. Tommy and Bunnie, her son and daughter-in-law, married when they were only nineteen. Bunnie became a stay-at-home mom to the son and daughter born soon after the marriage, while Tommy went on to college. But within a few years, Bunnie was tired of Tommy's spending long hours away from home because of his job and classes. Was he expecting her to do all the child-rearing by herself? Tensions mounted. A divorce seemed imminent.

"I drenched this deteriorating marriage in prayer and did everything I could to keep them together," Maria said. "I paid for marriage counseling, baby-sat so they could have romantic dates, and bought Bunnie new clothes. I even led her to the Lord."

The counselor advised Bunnie to leave the state and start over, which devastated Maria. "God, you know I don't want them to move," she prayed. "How can I give up my precious grandchildren? But Lord, I want your will, for I know that's best."

She felt God whisper to her heart, *Let her go; I am going to bless her.*

With that, Maria gave her blessing and told Bunnie she felt God would bless her future. As Bunnie sold their house and packed up to move, Maria thought of ways to help. She bought games for four-year-old Tonya and six-year-old John to play in the car, and packed lunches and goodies for the trip. She saw them off with her prayers, love, and an aching heart. But she knew God was in control, and she did all she could to express love to Bunnie. Maria never took sides in the divorce proceedings, never talked against Bunnie to the children or to her friends and prayer partners.

As it turned out, the children stayed with their mother only a few years before moving back to live with their dad and be near their grandparents. In the meantime, Maria and her husband paid for Bunnie to go to college, and eventually she started her own business. God truly was blessing her. Later on she remarried and had two more children, but Bunnie knew she had a friend in her former mother-in-law.

When Tonya and John moved back to live with their dad, Grandmother Maria became almost a surrogate mother. She realized Bunnie had allowed them to return because she trusted her and knew that if the grandchildren ever needed anything, she'd be there for them.

"I learned that grandparents must make sacrifices," Maria said. "My son worked nights, so I often kept the children when it wasn't convenient. I laid aside most of my social activities for several years to be there for John and Tonya—driving them to school events and sporting activities, having them sleep at our house. The divorce wounded me emotionally, but I had to keep my eyes on putting the children's welfare first. I found that prayer and forgiveness are two essential ingredients to keep one going after a family is divided."

Grandmother Maria had another important goal: to see the parents and grandparents remain friends. And they did. Whenever Bunnie flew in to visit her children, Maria would loan her a car. When the children talked with their mom, Bunnie could tell by their conversation that Maria had not been speaking negatively about her.

Ten years after John and Tonya moved back to live with their dad, Tommy remarried and had two more children. Maria and her husband paid John and Tonya's college expenses. Both of them graduated and have successful careers. Tommy and Bunnie remain friends, and there is no friction with the new spouses on either side. Maria said the focus of her prayers was to see them all show respect toward one another. When Bunnie's new husband was reluctant to meet his wife's former mother-in-law, it was Bunnie who assured him, "When you meet Grandma Maria, you'll just love her." And he did.

"This isn't to say it was always easy on the children, shuffling back and forth," Maria said. "But they did adjust fairly well, and they knew their grandma was always there for them. Saturating a family in prayer in the aftermath of divorce is sometimes all a grandparent can do. The divorce was one of the most painful experiences we ever had to face, but God was faithful. I did get to see my grandchildren grow up, and today all of us are friendly to one another."

Not all families will come out of a divorce as smoothly as this one did, but Maria's story offers encouragement and hope that it is possible. Grandparents aren't always financially able to help their grandchildren in as many ways as these were, either. But God is able to supply what is needed in response to prayer.

Dealing with the Pain

Children of divorce may view the breakup of the home as the biggest thing that has ever impacted them. Often they feel they can't talk to one parent without betraying the other. Grandmothers need to let their grandchildren know they can talk to them anytime, anywhere about the emotional roller coaster they are experiencing. Even if they can't supply satisfactory answers—which often is the case—listening is important.

In the *The Grandmother Book*, Jan Stoop and Betty Southard share the story of a grandmother desperately wanting to console her sobbing three-year-old granddaughter whose parents were divorcing. But her attempts to soothe the child—who was curled up in a ball on the floor—were met with outbursts of anger. Finally she stretched out beside her on the floor and lay there quietly until the sobs subsided. Then she said, "Hey, kid, let's go make some popcorn." Talking wasn't the solution at that moment, but Grandma's quiet presence was a calming influence. The authors write:

> There is no comfortable place for children who are experiencing the separation or divorce of their parents. It's as if they were living on a bridge; they don't belong on either side of the stream. And because they don't belong on either side, they often end up building their own little house of protection somewhere on that bridge, somewhere secret from those who are on either side. Even Grandma might not be allowed into that house, especially if she gets involved in the fight. On the other hand, if Grandma is safe enough to trust, she may be the only one allowed in.
>
> It's hard to stay out of the fight. You see things, and you understand things. But remember, more than anything else, children caught in a fighting family need a safe place. They need adults who can be there in the bridge house with them.[2]

Sometimes it's a real test for Grandma not to take sides if her grandchildren want to talk about one parent or the other, or a step-parent. But when we listen with sensitivity, it builds their confidence that they can trust us. We are conveying the message, "This is a safe place. I will keep our talk confidential."

The Power of Grandmother's Love and Prayers

Margaret is a typical grandmother who was enthralled with her first grandchild, a beautiful little girl named Sherry. Since her son's job kept him on the road living out of motels a lot, for two years his wife, Sonja, and the baby frequently stayed with Margaret and her husband, Bill. Gradually, the strain of separation and other family problems caused the marriage to deteriorate. Not long after their second granddaughter was born, things went from bad to worse. The young couple divorced, and Sonja left with the two girls.

"There were long periods of time when none of us knew the whereabouts of Sonja or the children," Margaret said. "During the three years this went on, God began teaching me how important a grandmother's prayers are. I was praying for the children one day (or maybe just grieving) when God interrupted me. In my heart I heard him say, *If you really are concerned about the children, you need to be praying for their mother.*

"I immediately replied, *God, don't you know she deeply wounded my son, betrayed our trust, and is exposing the children to unthinkable dangers? And I'm supposed to be praying for her?*"

Margaret said she felt God respond, *Yes . . . after all, she is their mother.* Though she hated to admit it, she knew God was right. So she opened her Bible, searched for pertinent Scriptures, and began paraphrasing them into prayers. During this time, Sonja occasionally contacted Margaret and Bill from a pay phone, but the only address she ever gave was the name of the town where they could wire money to her.

"God had given Bill the wisdom to realize it was important, for the sake of the children, to keep the lines of communication open," Margaret said. "Some may have said we were allowing ourselves to be used, but we knew we were following God's instructions. One time when she called, I convinced Sonja to give me a general delivery address so I could write to her. I sent her the paraphrased Scripture prayers and told her if she would start praying these daily, things would start turning around for her."

Later, Margaret learned that her daughter-in-law carried that letter in her purse everywhere she went. Her friends would make fun of her for reading it, but she would tell them, "No, I know this is real, and these prayers work."

"I told her that Bill and I loved her, would do anything we could to help her get her life back together, and that she was welcome to come home anytime," Margaret said. "By this time God had given me a supernatural love for Sonja. He showed me that she truly loved her daughters and that he would be able to use that love to pull her out of the destructive lifestyle she had gotten into."

In the meantime, God gave Margaret an unexpected ally. One night out of the blue, she got a call from Sonja's sister, expressing her concern. She and her husband both felt that if Margaret and Bill were willing to take them, the children would be better off with them. Everyone seemed to sense an urgency about the matter. Margaret again let her daughter-in-law know she was welcome at their home, and the sister agreed to try to convince Sonja to accept the offer. Margaret shared the Scripture prayers with Sonja's sister so the two could pray in agreement.

"God is so faithful!" Margaret reported. "Once I began praying in accordance with God's will, things began to happen. Within a few months, Sonja and the two granddaughters were back in our home. During this same time, God gave me Scriptures to send to our son. I asked him to read them every morning when he woke up ... and he did. The same week that Sonja called and said she wanted to come home, our son also called and asked, 'Mom, can I come home for a while?' I admit I was a coward. I didn't tell him until he got there that we had extended the same invitation to Sonja before we knew about his plans."

This is not a Cinderella story. Unfortunately, although they tried for a while, the two were never able to put their marriage back together.

"It is not my place to judge or pass blame," Margaret said. "I do know that God's Word always works, and the lack was not with God. Sonja remarried a man from our town, so we've had the privilege of having our two granddaughters grow up living close to us. Hopefully, Bill and I have had some positive influence on their lives.

"When Sherry was about seven years old, I made an offhand comment one day that 'even grandmas don't last forever.' The terror-stricken look on her face arrested me; it was as if God clicked a camera to give me a snapshot of that moment. He wanted to show me how important my role as grandmother is and how much Sherry, especially, counts on me. It was an awesome 'God moment.' Now that she's about to turn eighteen, I plan to write her a letter to mark this milestone in her life and tell her how special she is to me. I continue to pray the Word of God for her, asking the Lord to guide her steps and keep her close to him.

"Our two sons and one daughter have given us nine grandchildren. Over and over again there have been instances when God has given me insight on how to pray for a particular need for one of the grandchildren or a specific word to speak to them. What a privilege to be a grandma!"

An Empty Nest Filled Again

Rena, a friend whose husband is in full-time traveling ministry, had just reached the empty nest years when she looked forward to joining him on most of his trips. Then she received a devastating phone call from her older daughter, Elaine.

"She told me her marriage was over and that she was leaving with our four-year-old grandson, Dylan," Rena said. "Since she had no place to go, I of course told her she could come home, which she did. She had to get a full-time job, and I was totally against putting Dylan in day care, so I became his caregiver from 7:30 A.M. until 6:30 P.M. every weekday. My husband and I felt our role during this season was to offer unconditional love to our daughter and grandson and to try to provide stability in their lives."

Rena's new role was not an easy one. Dylan resented his dad, yet he missed him. Traumatized by the divorce, he also was confused by the drastic changes that had come to his life. "Nana, when am I going home?" he would ask, followed by her efforts to explain that he and his mom could not go back to the house he had always called home. Then he would cry and say, "My mommy likes her job better than she likes me." Rena tried to comfort him, knowing his pain was real and that her explanations would never answer all his questions.

"At times, I resented having to take on this responsibility at this season of my life," Rena said. "Caring for a child is demanding, tiring, and a major commitment; it was hard to deal with my feelings while at the same time trying to offer support to Elaine and care for Dylan. My husband became a surrogate father for Dylan and for years entertained him with made-up stories of 'Bart, the back-yard blue jay.'"

When the weekend for his court-ordered visitation to his dad would come up, Dylan would cry for days ahead and make up reasons why he couldn't go. Then about three years after the divorce, his father was killed in a car accident.

"Dylan had a really tough year working through emotions that are hard enough for an adult to process, much less for a seven-year-old," Rena said. "Once, he wrote a note saying, 'My daddy got what he deserved,' and put it on the bulletin board in his room. After several months he wrote another note, which said, 'I miss my daddy.' It was a difficult time for all of us."

Toward the end of that year, Elaine met a wonderful man, and they were married when Dylan was eight. Of course, everyone had to adjust to the new situation, but Elaine's husband is a good dad to Dylan, and the three of them are faithfully attending church together.

"This young man has been God's gracious answer to years of prayer," Rena said. "The Scriptures I prayed and clung to over those four years were Isaiah 54:11–14 and Jeremiah 31:15–19, and God has shown himself to be faithful. Many times people would let me know God had put us on their hearts and that they were praying for us. Dylan, who is now thirteen, recently said to me, 'Nana, if it weren't for you and Gramps, it's hard to tell what I would believe.' That was music to my ears!"

One day after Elaine and Dylan had moved out, Rena suddenly sensed God's presence in her room. In her heart she felt the Lord say to her, *Thank you for carrying your grandson for me.* Then she was inspired to write this poem.

> Lord, You are near, just a step away.
> Quietly walking beside me day by day.
> Every now and then, I hear You
> Sweetly whisper in my ear—
> "Thank you, Rena, for serving,
> For holding my son dear.
> You carried him for Me in your pain,
> But I carried you both again and again."
> That season is past, but its mark will remain;
> Forever it's etched—love's sweet stain.

A Troubled Teenager

When a family is broken by divorce, the children sometimes have greater than usual problems when they reach their teen years, as Grandmother Diane discovered. Two of her grandchildren were split up when her daughter divorced, Patty staying with her mom, and Justin going with his dad. Diane regularly prays for all her grandchildren, but she focused especially on praying for these two during and after the breakup. Although Justin attended church with his dad and stepmother, when he got to high school, he dropped out and drifted away from the Lord.

One night Diane dreamed she saw Justin standing before a judge in a courtroom; he obviously was in serious trouble with the law. As she prayed about the dream after awakening, she felt God assure her that Justin would get into trouble but that it would cause him to turn back to the Lord.

More than two years passed. Then one day Diane's daughter called to say Justin had been arrested for having marijuana and drug paraphernalia in his car. Now in his first year of college, he was being tried as an adult before a judge, without a jury.

"The irony of his arrest was that the stuff the police found in his car didn't even belong to him," Diane told us. "It belonged to his stepbrother. But because there had already been so much bitterness in the family since the divorce, Justin refused to squeal on his stepbrother."

At first it appeared he would have to serve a jail term because of this loyalty. But his attorney appealed to the judge for mercy, told him that Justin was paying for his college tuition by working with his dad, and called character witnesses to testify on the teenager's behalf. Although his parents had been quite embittered toward one another, this crisis caused them to lay aside their differences. They pledged to the judge that they would offer joint support to their son and cooperate with the court in any way they could. In the end, Justin was given probation, making it possible for him to continue college without interruption.

"He has to go for random drug testing whenever he's called, and he's not allowed to drink or go to bars," Diane said. "Also, he has to report to a probation officer on a strict schedule. The judge told him if he violates the probation rules in any way or fails a drug test, he will go straight to jail. It's probably the best lesson in discipline he could possibly learn. I truly believe this scary experience will cause my grandson to turn back to the Lord as we continue to pray for him."

Overcoming Emotional Problems

Connie tells of how she became very close to her first grandchild, Stephanie, because she helped raise the little girl after her parents divorced. But at age thirteen, as Stephanie entered adolescence, she struggled with adjusting to a new stepfather and developed emotional problems. She began seeing professional counselors, who prescribed pills for her depression, and she became addicted to the medications. Then her mother and stepfather moved her thousands of miles away to a drug treatment center.

"All this time, I was praying for God to heal Stephanie emotionally and also to keep her safe," Connie said. "She chose to put herself in many really dangerous situations, but because of prayer, God never took his hand from her."

Connie prayed that Stephanie would keep in touch with her grandparents, and she did. Through her five years of wandering, no matter where she was, Stephanie would always call Connie and her husband.

"Through it all, I was able to trust God and to pray that his will would be done in my granddaughter's life," Connie said. "Prayer kept me sane and close to him. At age eighteen Stephanie became pregnant and chose to keep her baby. This little blessing has changed her; it is truly a miracle that God worked in this way. I praise and thank him for the many answers to prayer for my oldest grandchild."

Dealing with Bitterness

When Grandmother Blanche learned that her son and daughter-in-law were getting a divorce, she felt as though a knife had been run through her heart. But she knew the bitter split would affect her four grandchildren even more and that they would need her prayers now more than ever.

The three adult grandchildren grew extremely bitter toward their mother. Only the youngest, who still lived with her mom, remained loyal to her. One daughter, especially, hated her mother because of the hurtful things she'd said against the children's father in the court proceedings.

Blanche prays that God will guard and protect all her grandchildren, help them overcome their bitterness, and bring them back to a close relationship with him. Daily she prays Scriptures over them, inserting their names in appropriate places. Sometimes she paraphrases several verses into a prayer, such as this one from Proverbs 4:20–27: "Lord, may my grandchildren pay attention and listen closely to your words. Help them to keep your words in their hearts, for they are life to those who find them and health to a person's whole body. Especially help them to guard their hearts, for the heart is the wellspring of life. May they not speak in perverse or corrupt ways. Lord, please make level paths for them to walk on, and help them to keep their eyes upon you. I pray they will not swerve to the right or to the left and that their feet will be kept from evil. Amen."

Lynette hasn't seen four of her grandchildren in a dozen years because her two daughters got mad at her for remarrying several years after the death of their dad. The children aren't permitted to communicate with their grandmother in any manner, and her letters and packages to them are returned. After she had grieved much, the Lord seemed to ease her heart. *You can't quit living, so keep on keeping on with life,* he seemed to whisper to her.

She prays, "Lord, let there be a time when my grandchildren desire to see me. In the meantime, let them know how much I love them. My pressing desire is for them to know you and to spend eternity with me in heaven. I choose to forgive my daughters for allowing their bitterness to alienate my grandchildren from me. May there come a day when we will all be reconciled because of your unconditional love and great forgiveness extended to all of us. Amen."

When Death Comes

While divorce seen through the eyes of a child can be traumatic and tragic, a death may be viewed as doubly so. Children who have lost a loved one through death—especially a parent or a sibling—need our nurturing, our emotional support, our listening ear, our encouragement. But most of all they need our prayers.

We can become a stabilizing influence to make a lasting difference in our grandchildren's lives, as author Irene Endicott suggests.

Children, even young ones, can understand death when the subject is treated honestly and sympathetically. Answer their questions that way. Your grandchildren will mourn visibly for at least a year, then within, out of sight, for many years to come. They will need more grandparent hugs now and your encouragement to talk about their mother [or father or sibling] and remember the good times. Be upbeat about their futures, and assure their sense of well-being by demonstrating your love and thoughtfulness.

Above all, listen to them, not just to what they say but to their body language and how they say the words. Their fears and pain must not be rationalized or covered up, but addressed either by you, another family member, or a professional counselor. Listening is your gift to them at this terrible time in their young lives.[3]

Praying for Grieving Grandchildren

Grandmother Bernice and her husband, Henry, pray daily for their six grandchildren, but they target their nine- and ten-year-old grandsons for special prayer. Four years ago, Bernice and Henry's son was killed in an accident when he was still in his thirties.

"I ask the Lord to be a father to them, and I also pray that someday they will have a Christian father," Bernice said. "How-

Grieving Takes Time

It's important to remember that grieving takes time. Those who have been through the process offer these suggestions:

- Accept the reality of the death (or other loss).
- Experience the pain of grief.
- Begin to adjust to life without that loved one.
- Talk about the person when you feel like it (cry and laugh if you want to).
- Do something to memorialize the deceased (give a memorial contribution to church or charity, establish a scholarship in her honor, plant a tree, or start a tradition like celebrating that person's birthday each year).

ever, their mother is dating an unbeliever, which breaks my heart. On the weekends he comes to visit, she and the boys stay home from church. My grandsons have accepted the Lord and have been baptized, but now I see a struggle within them, since the new man in their mom's life doesn't want to go to church. I pray a hedge of protection around my grandsons daily and ask God to give them his wisdom."

Bernice and her husband get up at five o'clock every morning, take a long, brisk walk, and come home to pray together in what they call their morning huddle with the Lord. Then they eat breakfast. When any of the six grandchildren sleep over, they often join this prayer time.

"We pray on many occasions with our grandchildren," she told us. "And we're especially glad our deceased son's children still live close enough to visit us and that their mother lets them come!"

Ideas for Helping a Child Cope with Loss

Often a child may blame God, another person, or even himself for the death of a close family member. He needs constant reassurance that the tragedy was not his fault. If the loved one was a Christian, it is helpful to talk about his or her new life in heaven. Praying with the child through every phase of the grieving process is the most helpful thing a grandparent can do. Holding the child and letting him cry will provide comfort and companionship. Another consideration is encouraging the child to talk with someone who has suffered a similar loss yet come through without bitterness.

Talking about special memories helps a grieving child who is in a state of shock after the death of a close family member. Going through picture albums can help him reminisce about the loved one he has lost. Sometimes putting together a "memory book" about that person is an outlet for his grief.

Author Jay Kesler reminds us that grandparents have a unique opportunity to help the younger generation see mortality for what it really is, while measuring things with eternity's values. He writes, "We can point to a faithful God and say, 'I've lived a long life, I've had a lot of experiences, and I can tell you, you can trust God. You can believe in Him; He'll take care of you.' . . . As grandparents, we can gently usher our grandchildren into an understanding of death not as an end, but as a beginning—a doorway into eternity."[4]

As devastating as divorce and death can be for any family, we have a Savior who can ease the pain and comfort the broken-hearted. To help with the recovery process, we grandmothers can provide listening ears for those who grieve and offer our prayers to the one who has the power to bring healing.

Prayer

Lord, help my grandchild [name] cope with [his/her] loss. Be [his/her] comfort, [his/her] strength, and [his/her] peace. Help [name] not to feel abandoned, and let [him/her] know [he/she] is not to blame for the tragedy. Be close to [name] as [he/she] goes through the grieving process; may [he/she] come through this tough time relying more on you than ever before. Help me to find ways to offer unconditional love and comfort during this painful period. Give [name] your joy, I pray. Amen.

Helpful Scriptures

He has sent me to bind up the brokenhearted, . . .
to comfort all who mourn,
    and provide for those who grieve in Zion—
to bestow on them a crown of beauty
    instead of ashes,
the oil of gladness
    instead of mourning,
and a garment of praise
    instead of a spirit of despair.
          —Isaiah 61:1–3

> Blessed are those who mourn,
> for they will be comforted.
>
> —Matthew 5:4

For the Lord himself will come down from heaven, with a loud command, with the voice of the archangel and with the trumpet call of God, and the dead in Christ will rise first. After that, we who are still alive and are left will be caught up together with them in the clouds to meet the Lord in the air. And so we will be with the Lord forever. Therefore encourage each other with these words.

> —1 Thessalonians 4:16–18

Scripture Prayer

O God, have mercy on my grandchild [name]. May [he/she] take refuge in the shadow of your wings until the disaster of [his/her] loss has passed. Father, I pray that in your presence [name] will find fullness of joy [Pss. 57:1–2; 16:11].

Related Scripture References

2 Samuel 12:18–23
John 14:1–4
1 Corinthians 15:50–57
Revelation 21:1–4

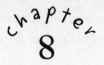

chapter
8

Praying for Adopted Grandchildren and Stepgrandchildren

For you did not receive a spirit that makes you a slave again to fear, but you received the Spirit of sonship. And by him we cry, *"Abba,* Father." The Spirit himself testifies with our spirit that we are God's children . . . heirs of God and co-heirs with Christ.

—Romans 8:15–17

How do you put broken families back together again? How can a group of individuals of diverse backgrounds, life experiences and ages ever become a family at all? I did not have the answers, but I knew Someone who did. . . . What a comfort to know that He has experienced what families are up against, sympathizes and stands waiting and available with the wisdom and help we need.

—Catherine Marshall,
The Best of Catherine Marshall

We may or may not be close to our stepchildren's children or to our children's stepchildren, but we can be motivated to pray for them because we know they are a part of our lives for a reason. 133

The same goes for adopted grandchildren. We can ask God to give us his heart and his love for them as if they actually were our biological grandchildren.

Stepchildren and adopted children often struggle to feel they're accepted by parents, siblings, and members of the extended family. Grandmother's loving concern and faithful prayers can be a strong, positive influence in their lives.

"We Embraced Her As Our Own"

Ruby told us that when she met her future "daughter-in-love," Sherry, and her one-year-old daughter, Chris, it was love at first sight. Ruby's son, Joe, married Sherry when the baby had just turned two, and they dedicated her to the Lord at that time.

"Chris was our first grandchild, and we looked on her as our family bonus," Ruby said. "Joe later adopted her, and we embraced her as our own. From the time we first met this child, my husband and I prayed every day that Chris would grow up to love the Lord with all her heart and with all her soul and with all her strength and with all her mind" (see Luke 10:27).

Perhaps the most famous grandmother in the Old Testament is Naomi. When both her sons died, Naomi probably despaired of ever having grandchildren. But when her daughter-in-law Ruth married Boaz and gave birth to Obed, her joy was full, even though the baby was not her biological grandchild. Scripture gives this account: "And the women of the city said to Naomi, 'Bless the Lord who has given you this little grandson; may he be famous in Israel. May he restore your youth and take care of you in your old age; for he is the son of your daughter-in-law who loves you so much, and who has been kinder to you than seven sons!' Naomi took care of the baby, and the neighbor women said, 'Now at last Naomi has a son again!'" (Ruth 4:14–16 TLB).

Naomi's stepgrandson did indeed become famous. He was the father of Jesse, whose son David became the greatest king in Israel. And through David's lineage came Jesus, the Messiah.

Healing Relationships

A blended family is incredibly complex because of the stressed emotional relationships. For children who've lost a parent, whether by death, divorce, or abandonment, the emotional wounds may cause repercussions for years to come. Forgiveness and loving acceptance are essential to keeping a blended family intact, as our friend Anna discovered.

When she married in her late thirties, Anna inherited two stepchildren—a nine-year-old boy and an eleven-year-old girl, both of whom greatly resented her. But gradually they began to call her Mom as they grew up. Later, they married and had families of their own.

Then shortly before Christmas three years ago, Anna and her husband suffered a serious car accident. He was killed in the crash, and she went to the hospital. During the following year, Anna struggled to recover from her injuries while also working through the grief of losing her husband. But she had another problem. Her stepson, Duncan, seemed consumed with old resentments and feelings of rejection from his childhood.

Their relationship became even more rocky when he tried to take over her house, but she insisted she wasn't moving. The following Christmas, she wrote both children a letter expressing her hurt and bewilderment because of Duncan's harsh attitude, which had negatively affected his sister. She signed the letter, "Your Stepmother." It was a wake-up call for Duncan. He called to apologize, and they talked a long time to air out the layers of anger and bitterness Anna didn't know he still felt.

"You are my mom . . . and will continue to be," he said at last. "Don't call yourself my stepmother again."

Upon talking to his children, Duncan realized that they, too, had been affected by his bitterness. Their relationship with Anna needed to be closer, and they took steps to keep in regular contact. Now Anna's three stepgrandchildren, ranging in age from sixteen to twenty-one, correspond with her frequently through e-mails and letters.

Each of Duncan's children has made a commitment to the Lord, and the oldest just married, adding a grandson-in-law to Anna's prayer list. All of them are thankful that through the years, Anna has prayed for them faithfully. She prays Psalm 91 for protection over them and prays they will be strengthened to stand firm for the Lord, no matter what circumstances they face.

"I'm glad God has healed our family," she said. "Otherwise, I wouldn't have a family or the joy of being connected with these grandchildren."

Cross-Cultural Adoptions

Jan and her husband, Chuck, were dismayed when their daughter, Roberta, single and in her late thirties, asked them to pray with her about adopting a baby. The couple did pray, but they were concerned about Roberta's spiritual condition. They felt she shouldn't adopt until the Lord had first place in her life so she would raise the child according to his principles, the ones they had taught her.

Then one day Roberta found herself in a hospital emergency room facing a medical crisis. In her heart, she called on the Lord and returned to the faith of her youth. Not only did her priorities change, but she also felt God healed her of her respiratory problem. Shortly afterward she started taking serious steps toward adopting; she especially wanted a little girl. This is how Jan and Chuck prayed:

- That Roberta would know with certainty whether adopting a baby was what the Lord wanted her to do as a single career woman.
- That God would open and shut doors as guidance for her.
- That if and when a baby was offered for adoption, she would have peace about it.

When she applied to a Christian adoption agency, the caseworker told her she might qualify for a biracial or African-American baby. Within six months—even before the home study and all the paperwork were done—Roberta received word that a black girl had been born. The infant was a few weeks premature, weighing only five pounds, but appeared to be healthy. The mother had terminated all parental rights. Doctors kept the baby in the hospital for a week to make sure she had no serious problems. Then Roberta received her daughter and named her Nancy.

"We knew this baby was an answer to prayer for our daughter," Jan said. "Later, the caseworker told us that when she learned this child was available, she felt the Lord say to her, *This is Roberta's baby girl.* She had prayed that she'd know the right home for this child; now she had peace that Roberta was God's choice."

Relating to Adopted Grandchildren

Here are some guidelines for relating to adopted grandchildren or stepgrandchildren:

- In your attitude, demeanor, and gift giving, cause each child to feel he or she is just as important to you as your blood-related grandchildren. A wise grandmother never shows partiality toward any of her grandchildren.
- Let them know you are praying for them and invite them to share prayer needs with you, assuring them that anything they tell you will be kept in confidence.
- Look for opportunities to heap praise upon them for their achievements and positive traits. Adopted children or stepchildren often have a strong sense of rejection, and they especially need your loving acceptance and reinforcement of their self-esteem.
- When you must deal with their bad behavior, balance your corrective comments by pointing out the things you appreciate about them.
- Ask God to give you favor with your grandchildren and the wisdom to be a positive influence in their lives.

Jan and Chuck began praying that their new grandbaby would be accepted by the entire family and not be hurt by racial prejudice. They even began praying that someday Nancy could be instrumental in reconciling the races.

"I prayed that we would love her just as much as we love our two natural granddaughters," Jan said. "The first time I saw her, I knew it would be no problem. She looked up at me with those big, brown eyes as if to say, 'Thank you for loving me!' She truly is a blessed, contented, peaceful baby who radiates God's love."

Jan prays the same prayers for Nancy that she prays for her other grandchildren—that she will grow up knowing who she is in Christ and never give in to ungodly peer pressure or worldly standards. She also prays Scripture prayers, such as, "May Nancy live a life filled with love, joy, peace, and all the fruit of the Spirit. May she turn her heart to God, to walk in all his ways" (see Gal. 5:22; 1 Kings 8:58).

This grandmother has written out some twenty pages of verses that she prays regularly for family members, especially her three granddaughters. "I take these laminated pages with me to all kinds of places—even the fitness center—so I can pray them during my extra time," Jan told us. "Sometimes God gives me ideas and ways to pray which I had not thought of before, so I keep adding Scriptures. For example, when one of the girls goes to the dentist: 'Lord, let your hand be with her and keep her from harm so that she will be free from pain'" (see 1 Chron. 4:10).

Praying for a Grandchild They'd Never Seen

Under normal circumstances, most parents are thrilled when they learn a grandchild is on the way. But in some cases, shock and dismay take the place of joy. Donna and Larry found themselves in this situation when their daughter Jo was raped by an older teenager who attended the church they pastored.

Agonizing hours of talking and praying followed. Finally the three agreed it would be best for Jo to go to a home for unwed mothers and give the baby up for adoption. This trauma took place in the mid-1950s, when it was socially unacceptable for a young teenager to have a baby out of wedlock, particularly the pastor's daughter. Not wanting to subject Jo to public shame, they chose not to press charges against the young man.

In the fifth month of Jo's pregnancy, Donna drove her daughter from their home in central Texas to a facility in Oklahoma. But the place was cold and forbidding, not at all like a home where a terrified teenager could find a safe haven. When Jo began crying hysterically, "Mother, please don't leave me here!" Donna knew they had to trust God for another solution.

The two got back in the car and headed home, with Donna praying, "Lord, please lead me to a safe place to leave my daughter for her to have this baby."

Upon reaching Fort Worth—a city unfamiliar to them—Donna began driving the streets as if she knew exactly where she was going. She turned down a street and saw a residence with a sign identifying it as a home for unwed mothers. Donna stopped the car and they walked up the steps to check out what was to become the place of refuge they were seeking.

"It wasn't home, but I had peace knowing God had directed us there," Jo told us, looking back on the experience. "Much kindness was shown that day to a scared fifteen-year-old and her mom. How grateful to God I am for parents who not only loved me but protected and supported me. They resigned as pastors of the church and moved to Fort Worth to be close to me through this ordeal. Dad was a meteorologist for the United States Weather Bureau, so he got a job transfer to Fort Worth, teaching new recruits. But he continued to minister on a volunteer basis in small churches over a ten-state area."

Before giving birth, Jo signed papers giving up her baby for adoption. On the advice of the home's directors, she agreed not to see the baby after it was born and not to ask about its sex or any other details. At the time, most adoption agencies believed the less such a teenager knew about her child, the easier it would be for her to forget the whole thing and get on with her life. Although Jo agreed to this arrangement, she never, ever forgot the experience, nor did her parents.

"I always felt that I'd had a little boy, but I sometimes wondered whether he had lived or died," Jo said. "Mom never talked about it very much, but Dad believed the child was a boy, and that he did live. He and Mom prayed daily that their grandson would one day come to know Jesus as Lord and Savior."

Of course, rumors about Jo followed her to Fort Worth. Two and a half years later, when a young man named Darrell asked Jo about the gossip he'd heard, she told him the whole story. But that didn't dampen his love for her. The couple soon married and moved away for Darrell to finish college. The birth of Jo's first child remained a secret known only to her husband, her parents, and her older sister.

Donna and Larry took pleasure in the birth of other grandchildren and prayed faithfully every day for each of them. But they always included Jo's firstborn in their prayers. One day, on the birthday of this child, Larry shared his heart with Jo's sister. "Remember that you have a twenty-one-year-old nephew out there somewhere in this world," he told her. "I believe one day he will try to find his birth family. When that happens, I hope you'll be a support to your sister."

Seeing God's Faithfulness

Years went by, and Jo's three younger children grew to adulthood. When Larry died at age eighty-seven, the family discovered Donna had developed Alzheimer's disease, and they placed her in a nursing home. In this life, these grandparents enjoyed no fruit from their years of prayer for a grandchild they had never seen.

Then one day when Jo had a lunch date with one of her daughters, Laurie, she suddenly felt compelled to reveal her long-hidden secret. These two had struggled for years with a strained relationship. But as Jo opened her heart to Laurie that day and shared the pain of her past, mother and daughter quickly developed a deeper love and understanding.

Late that night, Laurie went on-line and began searching the internet for a clue about this half-brother she'd just learned about.

At two o'clock the next morning, after going through more than a hundred listings, she found a posting that seemed to align with all the facts Jo had given her, including date of birth, the age of his mother at birth, and the fact that she was part Cherokee. The posting also noted that the young woman was a gifted pianist and that her father was a pastor. "I've enjoyed a great life—am married with five children," the message concluded. He signed his name Michael and said he now lived in Fort Worth. The posting had been placed on the internet only nine days before!

Laurie called her mom with the amazing news, and Jo gave her permission to post an anonymous message. Soon e-mail was flying back and forth between Laurie and Michael, and Jo told her other children what was going on. Then Jo's husband, Darrell, sent this message: "Michael, we are aware of the many times God has directed our lives, and we are not totally shocked by miracles. I count the incredible timing of this series of events as just that!"

Immediately a reply came: "You really put me at ease . . . I am the only one in my adoptive family who is a Christian. What a joy to know that God took lemons and turned them into lemonade! I pray now that God's love and comfort will be with Jo and she will finally put the past aside and rejoice that God is always in control. Think of Joseph in Egypt. I like the verse, 'You meant evil against me; but God meant it for good'" (see Gen. 50:20).

After receiving some emotional healing, Jo began communicating directly with Michael. Finally the day came when the whole family gathered and she met her forty-two-year-old son for the first time. At last they heard the story of how God worked in amazing ways in response to the faithful prayers of two unrelenting grandparents.

Michael and his adoptive family had been living in the Middle East where his dad worked as a petroleum engineer, and while they were overseas, Michael's younger sister died. When he was seventeen, his family came back to the United States for a break. Grief-stricken and searching for answers, one day the young man wandered into a Christian bookshop in Seattle, hoping to be led to a book that would answer his questions about life. His family rarely went to church, and he knew nothing about the Bible. But the many prayers prayed by grandparents he'd never seen were about to be answered.

Walking the aisles of the store, he spotted a blue, denim-bound book called *Good News for Modern Man*. At the checkout, he discovered he didn't have enough money, but a kind woman standing nearby saw his dilemma and gave him the needed amount. Michael began reading the New Testament, in a modern translation, for the first time in his life.

He read in John 1:1 that the Word was God. A friend explained to him that "the Word" was Jesus. "I didn't know Jesus was God!" he exclaimed. He read verses which declared that Jesus was without sin. "I didn't know that either; I want to be like Jesus," he declared. When the friend told him he should ask Jesus into his heart, he replied, "I'll do it!" That evening, kneeling by his bed, Michael invited Jesus into his life. The next morning he was full of joy, and from that day on, his life was changed.

Today Jo enjoys a wonderful relationship with her firstborn son and daughter-in-law, as well as with the five grandchildren she never knew she had. "Through all these events, I've learned the importance of forgiving and believing that God can work even in the bad things that happen to us," she said. "God loves us more than anyone else ever could, and if our trust really is in him, then we must believe he has everything under control. Today we are rejoicing in God's answer to my parents' years of faithful prayer."

A First Grandchild Given Up for Adoption

Nora heard those usually thrilling words, "You're going to be a grandmother," under most unhappy circumstances. Her sixteen-year-old daughter, Colleen, was pregnant by a twenty-year-old who had already fathered another child. Nora and her husband, Bert, had begged Colleen not to date this young man because they knew he was not good for her.

Like many couples with a pregnant, unwed teen, Nora and Bert faced difficult decisions. Should the baby be raised in their home? Should the parents marry? Was giving the baby up for adoption a viable choice? Colleen never considered abortion because she felt that would mean killing her baby.

As the months ticked by, Nora battled her emotions. She resented the fact that Colleen was still dating the baby's father. She imagined her own future as stuck at home to help rear this grandchild while her daughter finished school, got a job, and eventually married. That could take from five to ten years, she figured. Was she up to it? Her other two daughters would soon finish school and be gone, but Nora would be tied down at home as a coparent.

She prayed desperately, asking God to soften her heart and provide answers to this dilemma. Meanwhile, Colleen was drawing closer to the Lord. Sometimes she'd write out Scripture verses that spoke to her heart and slip them under her mother's pillow. About halfway into the pregnancy, when Colleen decided not to marry the baby's father, Nora took her to an adoption agency for counseling.

Nora continued asking God to change her heart and attitude and to show each of them what to do. As she prayed and yielded to God's purpose, her attitude softened and peace settled upon her. At last she could say with certainty, "Lord, I'm willing to help Colleen raise this child for as long as he or she needs me. I'll do whatever it takes to pour love into my grandchild. I open my heart and home to my daughter and her baby."

Then a set of circumstances unfolded that Nora believes was God-ordained. Bert's aunt and uncle, who lived nearby, visited relatives in another state and learned of a couple in their extended family who had been married for ten years and desperately wanted to adopt a baby. They came home and told Nora and Bert about this prospect.

By now Colleen knew adoption was what she wanted. When she heard that a distant relative wanted her baby, she felt this was the right Christian family to raise her child. She and the baby's father signed adoption papers, and the six-pound baby boy was born that summer. Nora and Bert were to take the tiny newborn to his adoptive mother, who had flown in to get him. As they drove across the city, Nora held her grandson to her heart, sobbing most of the way. Bert was crying so hard he could barely drive.

"I felt the depth of the pain my daughter must be experiencing in giving up her baby," Nora said. "Once I'd held him in my arms, I felt he belonged there forever. It broke my heart to give up my first grandchild, but I knew we were delivering him to a new mother who had such longing in her heart for this baby."

Grandma's New Prayer Partner

The adoptive parents named him Kyle and agreed to exchange letters and phone calls with Nora and Bert. For the first two years, they felt they were in on everything—his first smile, his first day to crawl, his first tooth. They especially treasured the pictures of Kyle.

Colleen, still hurting from the pain of giving him up, didn't participate in the phone calls. But then she began to make tapes and write letters to be given to her son when he was older so Kyle would know how much his birth mother really loved him.

Meanwhile, Nora and Betty, Kyle's adoptive mother, were forming a strong bond by praying together on the phone for the baby. When Kyle was almost three, Nora told Betty she was planning to attend a conference in her state. Betty immediately invited Nora to come early and spend three days visiting their home to get acquainted with her grandson. The first night she was there, Kyle crawled up in bed with her to talk. Nora felt she had touched a little bit of heaven in getting to share hugs with her only grandson.

Over the years, Nora and Betty continued praying together on the phone for Kyle, and later for his adopted little sister. At age nine, when he attended a family reunion, he met his granddaddy, aunts, uncles, and cousins for the first time. And he met Colleen, his birth mother. One afternoon the two of them spent several hours together alone, talking and getting acquainted.

As Kyle grew older, he began to like school less and at fifteen showed signs of major rebellion. Nora and Betty prayed intensely for him over the phone many times. When he was sixteen, he was caught viewing porn on the internet. His grandmother stepped up her prayers for him, that he would repent and have a change of heart. His parents laid down the law: no driver's license or car unless he improved his grades, got a job, and changed his behavior.

Again God answered the prayers of a praying grandmother. Kyle's new girlfriend encouraged him to get back into church and to study harder. Today at seventeen, Kyle has a part-time job, his grades are up, he has a used car, and he's active in church.

Colleen married a wonderful Christian and gave birth to another son five years after she had given up Kyle. Grandmother Nora now has eight grandchildren, all of whom have a relationship with the Lord. She prays for them daily and keeps a journal of her prayers and how God answers.

A Divine Appointment

God's intervention in our lives often comes as a surprise. As King Solomon wrote, "There is an appointed time for everything. And there is a time for every event under heaven" (Eccl. 3:1 NASB). Sue's story is one of those God-appointed surprises.

It began at a memorial service for a grandmother who had died of a brain tumor. Because she enjoyed jazz and was such a fun-loving person, the grandmother's family held an outdoor jazz concert to celebrate her life.

Sue and her husband, Bobby, didn't know the family, but they went to the concert at the invitation of a friend whose son was playing in the band. Somehow Sue's eyes were drawn to a baby boy about one year old who was climbing the steps, trying to get up on the stage. She later learned he was the great-grandson of the deceased.

Sue watched as the baby's mother went after him, scooped him up off the stairs, and hugged him tightly. He was laughing gleefully, and the mother laughed back.

"Their mother-child bond was so sweet and beautiful—almost sacred—that my heart melted," Sue said. "It was like he totally trusted his mom. She would keep him safe but let him enjoy life to the fullest. I turned to my husband and said, 'That's about the most beautiful baby I've ever seen,' and he agreed."

Right then, Sue prayed silently, "Lord, I want that for our son, Matt. I want him to have a wife like that and a baby like that." Matt was twenty-four, had been on overseas missions trips, and was a budding musician.

Six weeks later, Matt came to Sue and said, "Mom, I met a girl last night, and I think she's the one."

"Tell me about her; what makes her so special?" Sue asked.

As they talked, he blurted out, "Mom, you will really like this part. She has a baby." The next evening he brought the girl by to meet his parents. She was the same girl Sue had seen at the concert!

"I wasn't shocked, just very happy," Sue said. "But I played it cool. I knew it was better to stay out of their relationship and not try to interfere. They dated, got engaged, and were married a year and a half later, when Conner was three years old."

All the time, Sue and her husband were falling more and more in love with this child. "He has brought more joy into our lives than we could have imagined," she said. "Though we have two other children, Conner is our only grandchild. We pray for him, love him, and can barely wait the six weeks between visits when we drive for six hours to go see him."

Bobby, the grandfather, has battled cancer and had an arm amputated and recently had to place his mother in a nursing home. With all the heartache their family has gone through, Sue and Bobby see Conner as God's special gift of joy to them. His laughter, his sensitivity to people with special needs, and his boyish enthusiasm have given these grandparents a new lease on life.

Matt has produced several music albums, and Conner has learned the words to every song. His favorite is the one Matt wrote for Sue, which says, "You will one day be grandma to my own baby boy." Every time he hears it, Conner shouts, "That's me, that's my song!"

Our friend Laura has five stepgrandchildren who don't live nearby, so she sees them only occasionally. But her prayer for them is, "Lord, if you have something to say to these grandchildren through me, please show me what it is. Then provide the right opportunity for me to speak to them. Otherwise, I put them in your hands, asking you to minister to them in your most effective way."

Whether our grandchildren are blood related or not, we grandmothers have the joy to pray for them, as we've seen from the stories in this chapter. In so doing, we share in the miracle of families born not of flesh and blood but of commitment and sacrifice.

Prayer

Thank you, Lord, for the grandchildren in my life, even those who are not my biological ones. I pray they will grow and mature to be all you intend them to become. I ask you to meet their needs in every area of their lives—spiritually, emotionally, physically, and financially. Help me to be a good example to them. I bless you, Lord. Amen.

Helpful Scriptures

Because of the LORD's great love we are not consumed,
    for his compassions never fail.
They are new every morning;
    great is your faithfulness.

—Lamentations 3:22–23

Set a guard over my mouth, O LORD;
    keep watch over the door of my lips.

—Psalm 141:3

If it is possible, as far as it depends on you, live at peace with everyone.

—Romans 12:18

Love is patient, love is kind. It does not envy, it does not boast, it is not proud. It is not rude, it is not self-seeking, it is not easily angered, it keeps no record of wrongs. Love does not delight in evil but rejoices with the truth. It always protects, always trusts, always hopes, always perseveres. Love never fails.

—1 Corinthians 13:4–8

Scripture Prayer

Lord, I pray for the parents who raise these special grand-children [names], that you will give them wisdom—heavenly wisdom that is pure, peace-loving, considerate, submissive, full of mercy and good fruit, impartial, and sincere. Help me and also the parents to be peacemakers who sow in peace and raise a harvest of righteousness in the younger generation [James 3:17–18].

Related Scripture References

Matthew 18:1–10; 25:40
John 10:10–11
1 Timothy 1:1–2, 18
2 Timothy 1:2; 2:1
Titus 1:4
Philemon 10

Praying for Prodigal Grandchildren

If you know people who have wandered off from God's truth, don't write them off. Go after them. Get them back and you will have rescued precious lives from destruction and prevented an epidemic of wandering away from God.

—James 5:19–20 MESSAGE

All is not lost when our children make foolish choices. It will be painful for us to watch them eat hog's food, but there is hope that when that happens they will learn from experience what they never could have learned from precept.

—John White, *Parents in Pain*

Are you brokenhearted because one or more of your grandchildren is a prodigal, because he or she has chosen to leave the Father's house for the "far country"?

In talking to grandmothers around the country, we've discovered that quite a few seem reluctant to say they have wayward grandchildren. In some cases, they feel so distant from their grandchildren's everyday lives that they're not really sure about their 149 spiritual condition. Perhaps the children's parents keep the grand-parents from knowing all that's going on in their youngsters' lives because of their own sense of failure.

Realistically, we may need to ask ourselves, "Am I ashamed to admit that my children's offspring turned out to be less than the perfect kids I had envisioned?" If parents and grandparents alike can lay down their pride and discuss such issues openly, they can form a powerful team to pray in agreement for the wandering one to return.

Even if our grandchildren didn't receive Christian nurturing as they grew to adulthood—and even if they are adopted grand-children or stepgrandchildren—we still can claim them as part of our righteous seed that will be delivered (see Prov. 11:21 KJV).

As we seek his guidance, God will show us how to pray effectively, whether our grandchildren are trapped by negative peer pressure, addictions, sexual sin, occult involvement, materialism, or a host of other pursuits. He also can show us how to reach out to them with unconditional love. This means loving no matter what, loving without hope of receiving love in return, loving despite bad behavior. Unconditional love doesn't cut the person off when love is not reciprocated.

God Will Never Let Her Go

Marlene's twenty-four-year-old granddaughter, Kim, has been a longtime prodigal, but this grandmother has remained her strongest prayer advocate. Though they live many miles apart, Marlene finds ways to keep in contact with Kim and express love to her.

"After Kim graduated from college, her life started going down-hill," Marlene said. "She overspent on credit cards and began doing heroin with her boyfriend. Her parents had moved away, leaving her on her own. She moved from place to place, sleeping anywhere someone would give her a bed, and lost weight because she wasn't eating properly."

Kim's parents had contact with her only by phone, so they were unaware of how desperate the situation really was. Then one day they surprised Kim by going to the city where she was living and confronting her. They were shocked to find her living in horrible filth. At their insistence, she entered a drug program.

Grandma Marlene contacted a few close Christian friends to join her in praying for Kim's freedom from drugs and for her return to the Lord. As a little girl, she had loved the things of God and once had prayed with her grandmother, asking Jesus to be her Savior.

"God in his mercy delivered her from the drugs," Marlene wrote. "She's not yet serving him, but God is so faithful, he will never let her go. She says I'm her most favorite person in the whole world. I know she sees Jesus in our home, and he is knocking at the door of her heart."

Kim works as a door-to-door salesperson and often is invited into a home where the occupants share Jesus with her. She always calls her grandmother to let her know when a Christian has encouraged her.

Marlene prays this Scripture prayer based on Psalm 119:33–39 for her grandaughter, substituting her name to make it personal: "Teach Kim, O Lord, to follow your decrees. Give her understanding; help her to keep your law and obey it with all her heart. Direct Kim in the path of your commands, for there she will find delight. Turn her heart toward your statutes and not toward selfish gain. Turn her eyes away from worthless things; preserve Kim's life according to your Word; fulfill your promise to her so that you may be feared. Take away the disgrace, for your laws are good."

Another is: "Then Kim cried to the Lord in her trouble, and he saved her from her distress. He brought Kim out of darkness and the deepest gloom and broke away her chains" (Ps. 107:13–14).

A Listening Ear

As grandchildren grow older and face the frustrations of conflict with parents, peer pressure, or problems at school, a grandmother can provide solace and a listening ear. Just having a trusted adult who will hear his heart and receive him with love, not criticism, could help prevent a young man from following the path of a prodigal. Barbara Johnson illustrates with this vignette:

Recently I heard someone reminisce, saying that as a teenager he had fled many times to his grandmother's kitchen after an argument with his parents. There he had found unquestioning acceptance.

"She never asked a lot of questions," the young man said. "She didn't take sides. She really didn't talk much at all. She just opened her door—and her heart—and took me in. Maybe part of the relief I felt by being with her was that my parents had always expected so much of me—and Grandmother expected *nothing* of me, except that I let her love me."

This grandmother had probably never read any of the self-help books that are out there these days, offering wise advice on how to reach out to teens when they're going through family crises. But she showed great wisdom in opening her heart and especially by *listening* nonjudgmentally.[1]

Prodigals Respond to Prayer

Author and Christian broadcaster Tom Bisset explores "faith rejection" in his excellent book *Why Christian Kids Leave the Faith*. He feels more people have wandered from faith and returned than many people realize; in fact, he says most of those who wander do indeed return.

After interviewing scores of prodigals to find out what made them stray, he came up with four reasons. His survey subjects told him they left the faith because:

1. They had troubling, unanswered questions about their faith.
2. Their faith wasn't working for them.
3. Other things in life became more important than their faith.
4. They never personally owned their faith; they had simply tried to conform to other's expectations of them.[2]

But the good news is that prodigals respond to prayer and unconditional love! We must be faithful to pray for them and entrust them to our Good Shepherd, who cares more deeply for wandering sheep than we ever could.

In his concluding chapter, Mr. Bisset drives home this encouraging truth:

> God is *everywhere* and . . . He is *always seeking* His own. Walking away from your faith is not simply a matter of washing your hands of God and all you have learned about Jesus Christ and the Christian life. You cannot simply decide that you want a different way of life that involves little or no regard for God and His eternal truth. It's not that easy.
>
> There is no escape from the God who is everywhere. He is there and He is ceaselessly calling His own back to the Father's house.
>
> It does not matter that these wanderers refuse to listen or that they will not attend church or that they become silent when the conversation turns to spiritual things. It does not even matter if they refuse to read the Bible or pray. What matters is that they cannot escape from the God who is everywhere and who is always speaking.[3]

We can attest to this statement personally and from interviews with many parents and grandparents who have seen their prodigals come home. These wandering ones could not escape a loving God who was watching over them and wooing them back to himself.

We urge you not to become discouraged by negative circumstances in your loved one's life. Keep in mind that the Holy Spirit works in the heart and in the spiritual realm to accomplish God's purposes. A prodigal's heart has to change first, then behavior will change. We must follow the example of the father in Luke 15:11–32, never giving up hope that the wandering one will return. It is always too soon to quit praying for a prodigal!

Much-Needed Encouragement

I (Quin) remember how disheartened my husband and I were years ago when we were fighting a prayer battle for prodigals in our family and weren't seeing positive changes. God sent Paul Bill-heimer and his wife, Jenny, to have a meal at our table to encourage us. This minister and author told us about his own prodigal wanderings and about his mother's "power prayers," as he called them, which turned him around. He admonished us to hold on to the promises God had given us concerning our loved ones.

I read and reread this passage many times from his book *Destined for the Throne:* "My mother used these weapons [mentioned in 2 Cor. 10:3–5] on me. I was as hostile to God as any sinner. I was fighting with all my might. But the time came when it was easier to lay down my arms of rebellion than to continue my resistance. The pressure exerted upon me by the Holy Spirit became so powerful that I voluntarily sought relief by yielding my rebellious will. The wooing of divine love was so strong that of my own free will I fell into the arms of redeeming grace. I became a willing 'captive.'"[4]

After that uplifting visit from the Billheimers, my husband and I renewed our resolve to continue praying prayers of agreement and to trust God for our unbelieving relatives. One by one they began coming in—even an aunt in her nineties received Christ just before she died. God's timing for bringing our prodigals home may not be according to our desires, but his ways are always best.

Bombarded with Love

Ellie wrote to tell us how grateful she is that her husband's grandmother loved her and prayed for her until she came to know Jesus as her Lord and Savior.

"When I married my husband—who was not serving God at the time—I married into a family of staunch believers," she said. "His wonderful grandmother surely must have prayed for the future mates of all her grandchildren from the time they were born. When she met me for the first time, I was a chain-smoking, bleached blond who was into astrology. As soon as she could get alone with the Lord, I'm sure she probably said, 'Father, this was not what I had in mind for my grandson for a life partner, but your will be done. We'll just work with what we've been given.'

"And work she did. She bombarded me with love and acceptance like I'd never received from anyone. Much later, I found out that no one in the family could say anything against me without a reprimand from her. About six years after I'd met Grandma Bea, while sitting in my car during lunch hour one day, I asked Jesus to come into my life and heart and make me pleasing to him. I had been taught that Jesus is the Son of God, and through reading a book about the end times, I realized I was a sinner in need of a savior. No one had ever explained the plan of salvation to me, but I instinctively knew that I must ask God to forgive me through Christ. After praying in my car that day, I had no doubt that I was gloriously forgiven and that somehow Christ was living in me. My life has never been the same."

About a year after Ellie came to the Lord, Grandma Bea passed away, but the effectiveness of her prayers continued. Three years later, her grandson, Ellie's husband, recommitted his life to Christ. Now Ellie and Ron are praying for their own grandson who is a prodigal.

"We're praying he will come to the end of himself through the consequences of his sin," she said. "But we're also asking God to protect him from self-destruction. Before he became a prodigal, I felt the Lord gave me a verse for this grandson: 'No eye has seen, no ear has heard, no mind has conceived what God has prepared for those who love him' [1 Cor. 2:9]. I believe that when he does return to the Lord, God will pour out blessings on him that cannot be measured."

Persistent Prayer Is Not in Vain

Sometimes family members wait years for a prodigal to turn his heart toward God and come home with true repentance, not just regret and remorse. In the following story, it's a grandson who hears the voice of the Holy Spirit prompting him that the time is ripe to call his wayward uncle. A momentous decision changes the prodigal's life and impacts an entire family who had spent years praying for this dramatic turnaround.

Our friend Pastor Gregg Headley told us how his grandparents' prayers made a lasting impression on him when he was a child and would visit their home.

"Granddaddy and Granny Horton would call all of us to the living room at prayer time, and we all knelt as he prayed aloud," Gregg said. "Whether we participated or not, we definitely heard him pray as he offered thanks to God, then mentioned all the members of the family. But with special fervor and often with tears, he would pray for his prodigal son, my uncle Wayne, asking God to bring him back to fellowship with him. Never once in all the years of my visits did he fail to pray for this son, whose life was being destroyed by alcoholism. Granny told me that many mornings she found Granddaddy's pillow wet with the tears he'd wept while praying during the night."

Years passed. Wayne's wife developed cancer and was given little hope for recovery. Even in his prodigal state, Wayne knew the power of prayer, so he asked a local pastor to come and pray for his ailing wife. Since the couple didn't attend his church, the pastor refused the request, which of course only made Wayne more bitter. But God intervened by sending two ladies from the community whom they didn't even know to show unconditional love to Wayne and his wife as she was dying. They brought food, helped with chores around the house, and then, unperturbed by Wayne's coarse language, prayed. The prodigal's heart began to soften.

"My mother—Wayne's sister—tried more than any other member of the family to talk to her brother about the Lord," Gregg said. "But he always put her off by saying, 'No, not yet ... it's not time.' Then one day my brother, Bruce, was driving in his car and felt that the Lord spoke to him to phone Uncle Wayne, which he purposed to do as soon as he got home. But the still, small voice was insistent: *Call him now.* Bruce pulled off the road and made the call on his cell phone. He said, 'Uncle Wayne, I feel the Lord just told me to phone you and tell you that now is the time for you to make peace with God. It's time to come home to him.' Wayne's heart was ready, and Bruce led him to the Lord over the phone."

The grandfather didn't live to see his prayers answered, but his tears and intercession were not wasted. God used his grandson to lead the prodigal home, and Granny Horton, who is still alive, had the joy of seeing the fruit of their prayers.

Wayne lived for only one year after he came back to the Lord, but in that short time, his life changed in every possible way. He worked as a mechanic at a local auto repair shop, and his coworkers and customers would ask, "What happened to Horton? He's changed." He began attending church, and his pastor said Wayne probably shared about the Lord with more people during that year than most folks do in a lifetime.

"My mom was with Uncle Wayne shortly before he died," Gregg said. "His last words to her were, 'Be sure and tell Bruce how thankful I am for that phone call.' I can imagine the joyous reunion that took place in heaven when Granddaddy welcomed his son home. This example of the incredible power of Granny's and Granddaddy's prayers has blessed and encouraged our entire family."

Our prayers and tears for a prodigal are never in vain, even when circumstances may appear very discouraging. If we are faithful to pray, God is faithful to send his messenger to help turn our loved one's heart toward home.

Praying against Rejection

Phyllis and her husband, Art, pray together regularly for all their children and grandchildren. But for years they've focused especially on their prodigal daughter, Brenda, and her three children. Brenda and her husband, Monte, divorced when Kirk was three years old and Robby was not quite two. The third son was born later, the result of Brenda's adulterous affair, which had led to the divorce.

"As Kirk and Robby grew up, they tried to keep in contact with their father and visit him every summer," Phyllis said. "But Monte had remarried, soon had four other children, and was based on the West Coast as a trainer for the army. He managed to pay minimal child support but couldn't afford airline tickets for the boys to fly out from Virginia to see him. Sometimes he would promise them he was sending Christmas or birthday gifts, but they often came a month or two late. Monte seemed to want to stay connected, but he was struggling with financial problems, and Kirk and Robby felt he wasn't very interested in them. They suffered a lot of rejection."

By the time he was fourteen, Kirk had become very rebellious and angry and already had a drinking problem. Truant officers would find him drunk when they picked him up for cutting school, and Brenda felt she simply could not discipline him. In fact, he would become so angry that she sometimes was afraid of him. One summer she used her own money to send Kirk and Robby to visit their dad. When the summer ended, she talked to Monte about the discipline problems with Kirk, and he agreed to keep the boys with him.

"Monte is serving the Lord now and trying to be a good father to his sons," Phyllis said. "Not long ago, Kirk, now sixteen, stayed out all night and was picked up by the police. When they searched him, they found drugs in his pockets. My husband and I know that only God can heal Kirk's feelings of rejection, take away his anger, and change his heart. That's what we're praying for. Robby isn't really rebellious, but his relationship with the Lord isn't what it needs to be. We're concerned because he's so eager to be accepted, he'll go along with whatever his older brother wants. After this incident, Monte told us Kirk apologized to him for what happened and asked his dad to forgive him, the first time he's ever done that."

In the meantime, Phyllis and Art are encouraged that problems with Kirk have caused Brenda to turn back toward the Lord, and they see good changes in her. She seems to understand now how hurt and disappointed her parents were when she rebelled.

"She told us once that she had been afraid to come back to the Lord—afraid that she would fail him again," Phyllis said. "Recently Art prayed with her on the phone about her struggle with guilt over things she's done and her sense of failure as a mother; it was a real breakthrough that she allowed him to do that. We talk to

Brenda often to tell her how much we love her and to assure her that we're praying with her for Kirk."

Art talked to his grandsons several weeks ago about their poor performance in school. "I think you guys can do a lot better than you think you can," he told them. "I'm challenging you to work on improving your grades. For every A you make next semester, I'll give you twenty-five dollars, and for every grade that comes up a whole letter, I'll give you ten dollars."

They're responding to the challenge, to the delight of their parents and grandparents. "Dad, it looks like this is going to cost you quite a bit," Brenda told Art recently when she shared the progress reports she'd received on both boys.

The circumstances in this family have been heartbreaking at times, but Phyllis and Art are convinced that God is at work to bring something good out of every negative situation. "I heard our pastor pray one time, 'Lord, preserve our children from the evil defilements of this world,'" Phyllis said. "We're praying that for all our grandchildren."

A Covenant-Keeping God

In our book *Praying Prodigals Home*, we share the story of a minister whose daughter became embittered after her husband had an affair and left her with two children. She cut herself off from her parents and wouldn't allow them to see their granddaughters. But this minister and his wife put their faith in God's promises about keeping covenant with his people, and they prayed daily for their daughter and granddaughters based on these Scriptures:

> Know therefore that the LORD your God is God; he is the faithful God, keeping his covenant of love to a thousand generations of those who love him and keep his commands.
>
> —Deuteronomy 7:9

"As for me, this is my covenant with them," says the LORD. "My Spirit, who is on you, and my words that I have put in your mouth will not depart from your mouth, or from the mouths of your children, or from the mouths of their descendants from this time on and forever," says the LORD.

—Isaiah 59:21

By the time the girls reached their teens, the daughter was in financial trouble and asked her parents for help. They moved a mobile home onto their property for the three to live in and at last got reacquainted with their granddaughters. One day when the minister came home from a trip, he started up the steps of the mobile home to see the girls. But when he heard loud voices inside, he hesitated and listened.

"Why is it we suddenly have to start reading the Bible and going to church?" one teen shouted at her mom. "You've never cared about religious things before."

"Well, God has a covenant with your granddaddy, and we can't get out of it," she shouted back.

"A covenant . . . what's that?" the teen asked.

The minister quickly retreated, not wanting to interrupt their conversation. He concluded his story by saying, "My daughter isn't yet in the place I desire her to be spiritually, but she and the girls are on the way. It's a start. I'm trusting God to keep his covenant with me for our family."[5]

Forgiveness Is Necessary

Grandmother Edith wrote us of the heartache she and her husband feel because of a prodigal granddaughter, whom they've prayed for for years.

"Recently the Lord spoke to me about the necessity of forgiving Lucy," she said. "My husband struggles with this because he has the idea that if he forgives her, it means he condones the life she is living. We haven't seen or heard from Lucy since she came to our house for a family dinner three months ago. She was so quiet and withdrawn, my heart really went out to her. I wasn't able to talk to her one on one, but just remembering how unhappy her eyes looked makes me feel sad for her. When she was little and a preteen, she was such a happy-go-lucky kid. God is helping me to truly forgive her, and I'm praying my husband also will see his need to forgive her. I'm asking God to give Lucy a desire to return to the joy which she once knew in him."

An important key in praying for prodigals is not to judge them or hold unforgiveness against them but to pray with faith that their eyes will be opened to God's truth. Family members often suffer a lot of disappointment and loss in the aftermath of a prodigal's leaving, and forgiveness isn't easy. But forgiving doesn't mean condoning. To forgive means

- I choose to release the person from my judgment.
- I choose to commit him or her into God's hands, asking him to deal with the person in the way he knows is best.
- if necessary, I apologize to that person for judging him or her unfairly, for hurting that person in any way, or for not setting a godly example before that person.

God's grace and mercy are able to reach the heart of the most rebellious prodigal, no matter how abhorrent a pigpen he or she may be living in. We can't afford to allow our unwillingness to forgive to stand in the way of his mercy (see James 2:13). Meanwhile, he can heal our hurts and give us peace and the assurance that he is at work in our prodigals' lives.

Carrying on the Legacy

Sid, a children's pastor I (Quin) met recently, shared how important his grandmother's prayers were in causing him to lay down his rebellion and serve the God of his childhood. He had always enjoyed a special relationship with this grandmother because he was born on her fifty-fifth birthday.

"Grandmother Mary was an awesome woman of God," he said. "Born in Scotland, she came from a strong Christian family and was a longtime Sunday school teacher. Because my mom had had six children in twelve years, and my dad was working and going to night school, my older sister and I were 'raised' by my grandparents on the weekends."

Sid grew up in a denominational church attending Sunday school and communicants' class, but he had mostly learned rules and rituals, nothing about a personal relationship with Jesus Christ. Once he left home for college, he decided to run away from God.

"During my prodigal years, my grandmother was the main prayer warrior and constant intercessor for my salvation," he said. "I went on to graduate school, where I met a young woman who witnessed to me of her faith and truly was a model of Christianity. On my grandfather's birthday, I accepted Christ as my Lord and Savior. Later, the young woman who had discipled me became my wife.

"About a year after I came back to the Lord, Grandmother Mary died with cancer. Some time later, my grandfather told me that she had prayed for my salvation every single day. He said she'd always had a secret desire for her only son—my dad—to go into full-time ministry. Well, it missed a generation. But I am now a children's pastor, seeking to raise up young soldiers for the Lord from among our youth. I am carrying on the legacy of my grandmother and fulfilling her hope to have a son in the ministry."

One grandmother wrote how she prays for a grandson held in a detention center: "Lord, I pray you will send your Holy Spirit to give my grandson comfort when he is feeling down and missing his family. I pray he will turn his heart back to you, Lord, that he will hear your voice and follow the plan you have for his life. I pray he will choose the right friends who will point him toward you. Help him to see he is abusing his body with his lifestyle of drug use. May the adults who are in authority over him give him wise advice with tough love. Lord, I pray for his complete deliverance from all addictions. Thank you in advance for the day he will come home a new creature, praising you and rejoicing over what life with you holds in store for him. Amen."

It's Always Too Soon to Quit Praying

We can easily become discouraged when we focus on negative circumstances in the lives of prodigal grandchildren instead of affirming our faith in God's Word. At such times, call to mind the record of God's faithfulness in the past and offer thanks that he is working in unseen ways to change the heart of your prodigal. Tom Bisset shares an encouraging story of a young woman named Darlene who left her Christian faith and pursued a life of lesbianism. God sent a godly counselor into her life, and her concern for a close friend caused her to start reading her Bible again.

"Even when I was doing the worst things, I never really ever threw my faith out entirely," she told Mr. Bisset. "While I had stopped going to church, I never said, 'Jesus Christ, get out of my life.' The things I had learned as a child were still there. . . . Two things, love and truth, coming together in my parents, modeled God for me. I'm sure it was a part of the reason I came back to my faith."[6]

Take heart, praying grandmother, and know that your tears and prayers will one day be rewarded.

Prayer

Lord, I'm grieved because my grandchild [name] has chosen to turn away from trusting in you, not realizing that [he/she] is now on a path of destruction. Help me to reach out to [him/her] with unconditional love; please send someone across [his/her] path who will speak the Word of God into [his/her] life with boldness. Lord, I choose to forgive [name] for disappointing me and for all the hurt [he/she] has caused others. I commit this grandchild into your hands and pray you will send the Holy Spirit to turn [his/her] heart back toward you. Thank you for your faithfulness. Amen.

Helpful Scriptures

This is what the LORD says:

> "Restrain your voice from weeping
> and your eyes from tears,
> for your work will be rewarded," declares the LORD.
> "They will return from the land of the enemy.

So there is hope for your future," declares the LORD.
  "Your children will return to their own land."

—Jeremiah 31:16–17

For with God, nothing is ever impossible and no word from
God shall be without power or impossible of fulfillment.

—Luke 1:37 AMPLIFIED

His divine power has given us everything we need for life and
godliness through our knowledge of him who called us by his
own glory and goodness. Through these he has given us his
very great and precious promises, so that through them you
may participate in the divine nature and escape the corrup-
tion in the world caused by evil desires.

—2 Peter 1:3–4

Scripture Prayer

*Keep [name], O Lord, from the hands of the wicked; pro-
tect [him/her] from men of violence who plan to trip
[his/her] feet. You are [his/her] God! O Sovereign Lord,
[name's] strong deliverer, who shields [him/her] in the day
of battle [Ps. 140:4, 7].*

Related Scripture References

Genesis 18:10; 21:1
Joshua 23:14
Job 33:14–18
Psalm 33:11
Luke 15:11–32
Romans 15:13
1 Corinthians 1:20–23

chapter
10

Praying for Choices and Turning Points

Trust in the LORD with all your heart and lean not on your own understanding; in all your ways acknowledge him, and he will make your paths straight. Do not be wise in your own eyes; fear the LORD and shun evil.

—Proverbs 3:5–7

What ultimately happens when our choices are linked to God's directives? . . . He offers His true and lasting support. He takes us at our word, and He weaves His power into the fabric of our lives. In place of our turmoil, He brings peace. Instead of our weakness and instability, He provides strength and stability.

—Charles Swindoll,
Dropping Your Guard

It is never too early for us to pray for our grandchildren regarding crucial choices and turning points in their lives. From our experience, we know how early decisions shape a person's life in important ways: choice of friends, educational choices, career moves, marriage partners, which church to attend.

Most of us, in either our immediate or extended families, have dealt with painful situations caused by young people's wrong choices: an out-of-wedlock pregnancy, a drug charge, a car accident caused by drunken driving, intimidation by gang members, failing grades due to negative influence of peers, school discipline problems due to rebellious behavior.

Sometimes grandparents tend to think they know how things should turn out for their children or grandchildren. But only God knows what truly is best for those we love. Let's ask the Holy Spirit to guide our prayers according to his plan for them as they make important choices.

Following Grandmother's Example

Grandparents often influence grandchildren in their very early years, though it may happen unconsciously. Jack Terry, a renowned Christian artist who paints breathtaking western scenes, is a good example. When he was only three years old, he sat at his grandmother's side and watched her paint beautiful landscapes and still lifes. Even at that early age he had a strong desire to draw and to imitate what she was doing.

As the years passed, Jack sought instruction and counsel from successful professionals. By the age of twelve he knew that God's plan for his life included painting. A verse of Scripture spoke to him: "In his heart a man plans his course, but the LORD determines his steps" (Prov. 16:9).[1]

Today, his paintings reflect the glory of God's creation. But who can deny the early influence of a wise and talented grandmother who encouraged a young boy to develop his gifts?

A Future of Hope

Our friend Laura grew greatly concerned when her grandson, Tony, became more and more dissatisfied with his engineering major in college. His parents had divorced, and he was frustrated with trying to please his dad, who was paying for his education and insisted on this career choice. Tony would sometimes drop a class when he just couldn't comprehend the subject matter, which infuriated his dad.

Grandmother Laura prayed diligently for this young man, whose first love was music. Tony played in orchestras in the summer and desperately wanted a career connected with music. After attending college for almost five years, he still wasn't even close to graduating, though he studied hard during exam time to try to finish his engineering requirements.

Laura always sent Tony a box of homemade cookies and a note of encouragement during exam week. But one spring term she enclosed this Scripture: "'For I know the plans I have for you,' declares the LORD, 'plans to prosper you and not to harm you, plans to give you hope and a future. Then you will call upon me and come and pray to me, and I will listen to you. You will seek me and find me when you seek me with all your heart. I will be found by you,' declares the LORD, 'and will bring you back from captivity'" (Jer. 29:11–14). Several phrases in the passage seemed to leap into Tony's heart: *plans to give you hope and a future . . . bring you back from captivity.*

That note from his grandmother was a turning point, giving him hope in his despair. Tony felt God was encouraging him to use his musical talents; after all, it was the Creator who'd given him those gifts. Soon after he turned twenty-one, Tony dropped engineering. He moved in with his mom, transferred to a university near her home to study music, and got a full-time job to pay his tuition. His goal is to play in the Atlanta Symphony Orchestra.

Grandmother Laura is so proud of Tony's progress in pursuing what he has loved since he played his first instrument in middle school marching band. And she hasn't stopped praying for him to achieve his goals.

Encouraging Their Choices

Children need room to explore possibilities to discover where their talents lie as they grow and develop. Surprisingly, they sometimes indicate what those talents are at an early age.

When our second daughter, Melody, told John and me (Ruthanne) that four-year-old Rachel wanted to learn to play the violin, none of us took it seriously. Members of the local symphony orchestra had visited Rachel's preschool with several instruments and allowed the children to try them. Rachel waited her turn to try out a violin and loved it, not even wanting to give it up for the next child to have a turn. She got in line for a second turn and again tried to hold on to the instrument once it was in her hands.

She went home from preschool that day and said, "Mommy, I want to learn to play the violin." Melody, who had been a music major in college, thought that because she was so young, it was a whim that would quickly pass. But it didn't. Rachel went around the house humming and playing her imaginary violin, insisting she wanted to take lessons.

Melody signed her up for group music classes at age five, and Rachel began learning the keyboard and some music basics. Before she turned six, she was taking private piano lessons and doing very well, but she still contended she wanted to play violin. Finally, Melody rented a violin, found a teacher, and started her on lessons when she was seven. To everyone's surprise, she took to the violin like a fish takes to water.

We prayed with Melody through these stages and tried to encourage her when she worried about the expense. Grandpa John even promised to help purchase Rachel's first violin when she had grown enough to get an adult-sized instrument. In the spring of her second year of lessons, Rachel heard about the local youth orchestra and wanted to try out. She was nine years old, the minimum age.

Melody asked us to pray, and she tried to prepare Rachel for the possibility that she might not yet be good enough to make it. The group plays standard repertoire, not simplified material for beginners. But Rachel sailed through the audition with no fear and was placed in the second violin section. Before she turned twelve, she won the position of concertmaster, playing first chair in the first violin section.

Lydia, Melody's ten-year-old, has been taking cello lessons and is now preparing to audition for a position in the same orchestra. If her interest persists, we'll help her purchase her own instrument when she's ready, just as we did for Rachel. And eight-year-old Joel has decided he wants to play the trumpet like Grandpa John does. For Christmas last year, John gave Joel one of his own trumpets and also gave him his first lesson. He's now studying with a teacher and practicing faithfully.

During that Christmas visit, we were treated to a recital with each of the children playing a piano piece, and Rachel and Lydia playing a violin-cello duet, accompanied by their mom. Grandpa John took the opportunity to talk to Rachel and commend her for her accomplishments. At the same time, he wanted to assure her that eventually she will probably enter a competition and be beaten by someone more skilled than she is. "But losing doesn't diminish your talent or your worth as a person," he told her. "As long as you do your best, you need never be ashamed."

"I don't know whether any of my children will end up with a profession in music," Melody said. "But the discipline and persistence needed to study and play an instrument can be applied to other areas of life, and that's good for them. Also, with all of them involved in music at home and at church, it's a cohesive force in our family."

The experts really don't know to what extent genes shape a child's choices. But it's interesting to note that Rachel's grandmother, who died when Melody was only seven years old, was an accomplished violinist. Grandpa John had his first trumpet lesson when he was eight years old, and he's enjoyed playing brass instruments throughout his lifetime. And now it appears grandson Joel may follow in his footsteps.

In a government survey of children ages nine to seventeen, more than 25,000 respondents listed music as the leading factor for staying away from drugs. Other responses mentioned most frequently included family and sports activities. "The words and actions of parents, or other adult influencers, are more effective than they may think in keeping their children away from drugs," said the director of the agency overseeing the survey.[2]

Praying in the Future Tense

Recently I (Quin) spent a morning with Virginia, an amazing seventy-eight-year-old praying great-grandmother, the acknowledged spiritual matriarch of a family that greatly reveres her. Virginia's five grandchildren and seven great-grandchildren frequently confide in her with their hurts and problems, knowing she first will pray, then share any insights she receives for them personally. They keep in frequent contact by e-mail, by phone, or in person.

Virginia admits she has a great sense of humor and loves to watch children. She compares it to watching a plant grow, bud, and bear fruit. This winter she is living with her son Dave and his wife, their son Mike and his wife, and their two children. It's quite a household with four generations living under one roof, and they pray together about everything that's going on in the family.

The other night when eight-year-old Jennie got a spanking for telling a lie, it was Great-Grandmother Virginia who had a long talk with her after her sobs subsided. "Let me tell you the story of another little girl who once told a lie and got a spanking," Virginia told her. "That child told a lie to cover her misdeed because she wanted her parents to think she was a good little girl."

Of course, the story was about herself, and because Virginia empathized with Jennie's dilemma, the child listened to her great-grandmother's counsel.

"I can identify with Jennie because I see so much of myself in her," Virginia said. "I asked Jennie how she felt when she told the lie, trying to discern what her emotions were in order to get to the root of the problem. After the talk, I was able to suggest to Jennie's mom a way she might rephrase her questions to Jennie, who is slower and more laid back than she is."

Virginia says God shows her how to pray for her grandchildren's and great-grandchildren's choices for the future. Sometimes while praying, she senses God's assurance of a good outcome in the life of a particular child, an outcome unrelated to the circumstances of the moment.

"In the middle of the night, I'll awaken with a picture in my mind and an understanding of how to pray for that child," she said. "I ask the Lord to show me how she is feeling, what her needs are, and how to pray for her future. I write it down and wait until the appropriate time to share it. I'll know when her heart is ready to receive the message."

Andy, one of her great-grandsons, struggles with dyslexia. Recently he was suspended for roughhousing on the school bus. As Virginia prayed about the situation, the Lord showed her that Andy's dad, her grandson, needed to give more attention to praying for this child. When she shared this insight with him, he agreed and now is much more aware of his responsibility to pray for his household. He went with Andy to see the school principal, and the boy has been reinstated in school.

Though Andy is in some special education classes, he is creative and inquisitive, Virginia said. Reading is a hard, slow process, but he retains what he reads. He has excellent verbal skills and an amazing grasp of the Bible for a child his age. He checks out science books from the library and recently enjoyed making a model of a volcano with his dad. On Saturdays his dad drives Andy across town for his great-grandmother to tutor him. She mainly spends time encouraging him in his talents and getting him to talk about his feelings and dreams. Schoolteachers and friends may see a slow reader, but Grandma Virginia sees his potential for becoming a scientist. And God has her praying for that dream to be fulfilled in the future.

"It used to be if I felt the Lord revealed something to me for a family member, I was quick and blunt with my advice," Virginia said. "I'd also give Scriptures to back it up. But now I spend most of my time worshiping and praising the Lord, and I trust him to speak to me in the night hours about specific prayer needs for my family."

Virginia's twenty-seven-year-old twin grandsons still tell her anything and everything, knowing she will keep their confidences. One recently married, and the other is in waiting mode, assured that his grandmother is praying for God to lead him to the right wife. The twelve-year-old great-grandson who lives in the home where she stays runs to her when he wants to get something off his chest. He doesn't want to go to bed with any wrong attitudes, so he likes having a chat with Great-Grandmother Virginia before turning out the light.

Does she have any advice for grandmothers? "These young-sters are all in training for their future," she said. "Listen to the chil-dren and ask them what's happening inside—that's the starting point. Then pray for them as the Lord leads. Most people want to deal with the result of disobedience, rather than probing for the reason behind it."

"God put a gift of wisdom into Mom," her son Dave told me. "All of us in this family depend on her for prayer and godly coun-sel—from my children and their children to my sister's offspring. We've been blessed to have her to pray for us."

"Waiting Prayers"

As we've interviewed dozens of grandmothers, we've marveled at the creative ways God leads them to pray. One person's style of praying may not appeal to another, but we can learn from and be encouraged by one another. Thankfully, there is no formula for how we should pray for our grandchildren. It's only important that we do!

Pat told us she prays many "waiting prayers" for her grandchil-dren's future decisions. She has written them on pieces of paper cut into the shape of an egg and placed them in her big family Bible. "Hatch these in your timing, Lord," she prays.

She got the idea from reading about author Catherine Mar-shall planting "waiting prayers" for her son when he was still small. She didn't go "digging them up" until he was well into college, but Mrs. Marshall was thrilled to realize God's response had far exceeded the prayers she'd written years before. Grandma Pat uses the idea daily to pray for her dozen grandchildren. She leaves those prayers for their future in God's hands until she feels the time is ripe to open the Bible and see how God has answered.

Sarah told us she prays for all her grandchildren as they choose friends, mates, schools, jobs, and ministries, and that they will joyfully enter into his plan for their lives. "God's Word promises that 'as the mountains surround Jerusalem, so the LORD surrounds his people' [Ps. 125:2]," she said. "So I pray every day that each one of my grandchildren will be surrounded by angels to protect them, a shield of favor, songs of deliverance, and his mercy."

Ten-year-old Julian wrote us about how he appreciates his grandmother's prayers. "My grandma tells me she has prayed for me every day of my life and even before I was born. I'm glad she's always praying for me, even if she doesn't always know what I'm doing. Once when I came back from a trip to California feeling upset, she sat down and talked to me, and then we prayed. I was able to understand what had happened to me on the trip and why I felt bad. I think I understand God better because she explains things to me.

"Grandma prayed for her son—my dad—to get the right wife when he was only two years old. Now I have a great, loving, and caring mom. Grandma says she has prayed for the right wife for me, too. I wonder what she'll be like. Hopefully, I'll be able to pray for my children the same way Grandma prays for us—to keep prayer going on for generations."

Significant Events

Sometimes when grandchildren mark milestones in their lives, we have the opportunity to exhibit special interest in the things important to them. Birthdays, baptisms, baby dedications, weddings, graduations, anniversaries, house blessings—all of these are events which families can celebrate together in establishing traditions to continue into the future.

Carol and her husband pray consistently for their nine grandchildren, but they take care to make each one's birthday extra special. "At our family celebration, we place the birthday child in the middle of a circle of family members," she said. "We ask the Lord to deposit his value of them deep in their hearts so they will always know his acceptance and love and walk in it. We keep our prayers low key but very specific, with lots of hugs afterward."

Carol hopes that when her grandchildren are grown they will cherish memories of their grandparents praying for them on their birthdays and that those prayers will continue to follow them.

Another significant event for grandchildren is the opening of school. I (Quin) have started a tradition of taking one grandchild at a time out for a restaurant meal at the beginning of the preschool year. There we talk about the year ahead, getting them excited about the new friends they'll meet, the new teacher they'll get to know, and all the wonderful opportunities that lie ahead for them. I always pray aloud before the meal and also ask God's blessing on the grandchild. Then I invite him or her to offer a simple prayer. Only the newest baby in the family hasn't yet gotten in on this event.

Dedication, Baptism, Confirmation

In biblical times, families celebrated feasts, holy days, and other special events in festive ways. In my (Quin's) family, we dedicate our newborn grandbabies to the Lord in one of our homes with the other set of grandparents and aunts, uncles, and cousins present. Papa LeRoy and I pray blessings for the baby's future, for his spiritual and physical development, for his provision and peace, reading pertinent Scriptures aloud. Then his parents and other relatives who wish to also pray. Once the dedication service is over, we have a party that the little cousins love, complete with refreshments, picture taking, and gifts for the baby.

This tradition originated when my husband and I invited my grandfather, an elderly, retired minister, to our Florida home to pray over our three children when they were very young. At the time, I didn't realize the significance of asking him to bless them. But because my granddad had performed our wedding ceremony, I wanted him to lay hands on our children and pass a blessing on to them. The photos of those occasions are priceless to me.[3]

Families have different traditions where dedicating or baptizing babies is concerned. In our (Ruthanne's) family, my husband was privileged to dedicate our oldest grandchild, Amanda, to the Lord when she was a tiny baby. The next two granddaughters, Rachel and Lydia, both requested near the time of their tenth birthday that Grandpa John baptize them by immersion. Whatever tradition your grandchildren's parents choose to follow, baby dedications or baptisms are great opportunities for you to be involved in their lives. And the photographs taken on these special occasions are treasures you and they will cherish in days to come.

Grandmother Elizabeth wasn't able to be present for her granddaughter's confirmation day, so she wrote a letter to mark the event. She shared it with us.

Dear Granddaughter:

Congratulations on your Confirmation Day. I would like to have been there on the day you made your initial step in your "quest" for God. Or perhaps it's more properly said when you decided to give attention to God's quest for you! It was a high and holy day. Promises were made by you and for you by those who love you. It is sort of like your marriage day, except it's probably more important. Life as God defines it is forever. If we are a forever people, that makes all the difference.

I have to come back again and again to the fact that God was in Christ, reconciling the world to Himself. The crucifixion and resurrection of Jesus the Messiah is the hope of all humanity at all times and in all places.

I have a favorite thing Jesus said: "Are not two sparrows sold for a penny? Yet not one of them will fall to the ground apart from the will of your Father. And even the very hairs of your head are all numbered. So don't be afraid; you are worth more than many sparrows" (Matthew 10:29–31). I really like that! Hang in there, baby girl, you are of more value than many sparrows!

Love and hugs and all that stuff,
Grandma Beth

Seeing the Answer to Their Prayers

LeeAnn and Gerald have only one grandchild, Kathryn, so when her parents divorced when she was very young, it was a wrenching experience for the grandparents. "I think the reason I cried so much at the time was because I was looking at the problem and not trusting the Problem Solver," LeeAnn said. "Our son and daughter-in-law were terribly young and immature, and they didn't communicate well, so the marriage didn't survive. Our son chose to step out of Kathryn's life, but we determined to stay connected with her despite all the obstacles."

The grandparents were able to take Kathryn to church as she grew up, and they began early on to pray paraphrased Scripture prayers over her. One favorite was, "The Lord will perfect that which concerns [Kathryn]; Your mercy and loving-kindness, O Lord, endure forever—forsake not the works of Your own hands" (Ps. 138:8 AMPLIFIED).

"For years we were involved in a weekly prayer meeting where we would write names of loved ones needing prayer on a bulletin board and all the participants would pray over the names," LeeAnn said. "We put Kathryn's name on the prayer list every week, asking God to watch over her life and provide a godly mate for her. Did it work? Today our granddaughter is happily married and she and her husband work with the youth at a very large church in California. She e-mails me every day to keep in touch and share God's blessings. Yes, prayer works!"

Wedding Prayer

When Kathryn got married, LeeAnn and Gerald had the joy of attending her beautiful outdoor wedding, and Gerald gave her away and helped officiate. He wrote this special prayer for the occasion, which he prayed over the couple after they had said their vows:

Father, thank You for the wonderful gift of love, for there is nothing in all the earth to compare with it. Love is the means by which You bind two people together to endure the heartaches and difficulties of life. And because of love, the joys and mountain peaks of life are incomparably sweeter.

Thank You, Father, for Matthew and Kathryn, and for Christ who lives within them. They stand before us equipped to live in a way that will honor and glorify You. Thank You for teaching them spiritual truths which have prepared them for this day and for the days ahead. Thank You for every person who has contributed to the solid foundation of their lives.

We pray You will grant these two wisdom and discernment beyond human understanding. May they always be wise enough to ask the question, "Lord, what would You have us to do?" May You grant them increasing faith, and may they be willing to have their faith stretched. May their marriage be a beautiful overflow of love from You, so that others will see Christ within them.

I pray You will help them to understand that every experience is always an opportunity to discover something new about You, as well as something new about each other. Surely as Matthew and Kathryn grow toward You, they will grow closer to each other. I pray You will protect their home, and that they will look to You as their Divine Protector and Provider. In times of need, may they always seek and follow Your guidance in seeing every need supplied.

We who witness their vows ask that heaven's blessings will rest upon Matthew and Kathryn—now, and in all the days to come. Father, keep ever before them the simple truth that You have put them together to bring honor to You. This I pray in Jesus' name and for His sake. Amen.

Look for opportunities to establish traditions in your family to mark milestones in a way your grandchildren will always remember. Let them know you care about their futures as you encourage them in making wise choices and help celebrate the turning points in their lives.

Prayer

Father, thank you that you love my grandchildren even more than I do. Please call each one of them to yourself. I pray all of them will choose to put you first in their lives and will grow into godly men and women. Lead them not into temptation, but deliver them from evil. Keep them safe from the evil one. Reveal your purpose for their lives, that they may live up to their full potential. Don't let them be deceived, but show them how to live in such a way as to find favor with you and with man.

Father, I ask you to prepare godly mates for each grandchild and also prepare them to be godly mates. I pray they will excel in school, in work, and in every aspect of life, bringing you honor in all that they do. Please show me specific ways to express love to each of them. Amen.

Helpful Scriptures

I have not stopped giving thanks for you, remembering you in my prayers. I keep asking that the God of our Lord Jesus Christ, the glorious Father, may give you the Spirit of wisdom and revelation, so that you may know him better. I pray also that the eyes of your heart may be enlightened in order that you may know the hope to which he has called you.

—Ephesians 1:16–18

Consequently, you are no longer foreigners and aliens, but fellow citizens with God's people and members of God's household, built on the foundation of the apostles and prophets, with Christ Jesus himself as the chief cornerstone.

—Ephesians 2:19–20

Be very careful, then, how you live—not as unwise but as wise, making the most of every opportunity.

—Ephesians 5:15

"Behold, the former things have come to pass,
    Now I declare new things;
Before they spring forth I proclaim them to you."

—Isaiah 42:9 NASB

Scripture Prayer

Lord, I pray you will help [name] not to be anxious about anything but instead to bring everything to you in prayer. May [he/she] always offer thanks as [he/she] presents requests to you. May your peace, which transcends all understanding, guard [name's] heart and mind in Christ Jesus [Phil. 4:6–7].

Related Scripture References

Deuteronomy 30:19–20
Joshua 24:15
1 Samuel 1:27–28
Psalm 25:12–14
Isaiah 30:21
2 Corinthians 6:14–18
2 Timothy 3:14–15

Taking the Role of Parent or Coparent

This I call to mind and therefore I have hope: Because of the LORD's great love we are not consumed, for his compassions never fail. They are new every morning; great is your faithfulness.

—Lamentations 3:21–23

One of the toughest aspects of grandparenting the children of divorce is the energy factor. Children were designed for younger parents, and at the age when most people become grandparents, we are not temperamentally suited for raising children and solving the problems parenting entails. We must depend upon God if we want to be up to the task.

—Jay Kesler,
Grandparenting: The Agony and the Ecstasy

More than ever before in our society, grandparents find themselves taking the role of a parent. The number of children living with grandparents grew from 2.2 million in 1970 to almost four million in the year 2000, according to the United States Census Bureau.[1]

Divorce, death, imprisonment, alcoholism, drug addiction, abuse, abandonment—traumas of every kind may leave children without a responsible parent. That's when grandparents often feel compelled to step in. In other cases, grandparents provide a home for their grandchildren for economic reasons. But for anyone taking on this awesome responsibility, a strong foundation of prayer and faith in God is essential.

Prayer Is a Lifeline

"Prayer is the lifeline that has kept me going through this grandparenting roller-coaster ride," Joy told us. She is a grandmother whose nineteen-year-old daughter, Melissa, had a baby out of wedlock at the end of her second year in college. Then she decided to marry the child's father.

"At first, I had to deal with the shock of the pregnancy, but when Carrie was born, I just fell in love with her," Joy said. "However, Melissa divorced Scott within a year because he was abusive and subject to uncontrollable fits of anger. She found subsidized housing through a program for battered women, and since the divorce, I've been a coparent to Carrie. This role has been unexpected, confusing, challenging, fun, and difficult—all at the same time. And it's kept me praying. It's tiring, too, because I work full time at a very demanding job."

In many ways, Joy felt she was still parenting Melissa, so helping look after Carrie was like having an additional child. She often worried about the child's safety when Scott had her for his court-ordered visitation weekends. It was a conflicting time, as Joy would try to keep from telling her daughter what to do yet be supportive and help with the baby while Melissa struggled to finish college.

"At a time of my life when I wanted to rest from child-rearing, I still had kids to deal with," she said. "Yet I love being able to teach and help bring up a little one again, and I try to pour into Carrie as much as possible when I'm with her. I'm continually reminded that life is from God, and I want to cherish this gift of joy and delight that he's given us."

Joy shared with us some of the things that have helped with her coparenting role.

- "Support from prayer partners, people who would really pray for Melissa and Carrie and me and who would listen when I needed to talk out my frustrations.
- "Taking time to be with the Lord, time for prayer and for listening to him.
- "Stopping for tea times when I could grab some quiet for reflection.
- "Releasing Melissa and Carrie to the Lord, not hanging onto the burden of it all. I couldn't 'carry' them and be available physically or I'd be totally exhausted. I had to trust the Lord for strength moment by moment.
- "Relaxing and flowing into his plan, learning to trust him even when I couldn't understand what was going on.

"I have prayed consistently for this grandchild her whole life, even before she was born," Joy said. "When she was only two days old, I held her and prayed God's blessings and protection over her. For three years she has struggled with asthma-type symptoms, but the Lord impressed me to pray a healing prayer over her every morning as I prepare for the day. She has done much better since the prayer has been consistent, and now I'm teaching her to pray the Scriptures on healing with me [Ps. 103; Matt. 8:17; 1 Peter 2:24]. I pray Psalm 91 over her for protection and declare that the Word is alive [Heb. 4:12], bringing soundness to her body. I speak this Word over her like I would give her medicine.

"When she was still a baby, I got into the habit of singing songs over her about the blood of Jesus, and now she knows all of them. The other day I looked in my rearview mirror and saw Carrie in the back seat of the car with her hands lifted and eyes tightly closed, singing 'there is a fountain filled with blood' at the top of her lungs."

Escaping an Abusive Husband

Maelynn, whose daughter ran away from an abusive husband after living with him for ten years, has had to adjust to having a little one underfoot again. The daughter, emotionally bankrupt, arrived with the clothes on her back, the baby wrapped in blankets, and little else.

"Coparenting at our age wasn't exactly easy," she wrote. "My husband and I were in our sixties, a time when we were looking forward to traveling. But suddenly we were helping to raise a baby again. When our daughter was sufficiently healed from her trauma, she found a job, but she couldn't earn enough to move out. Her husband paid no child support. All her money seemed to go to day care or to pay attorney's fees and court costs to keep the child in her custody. Four years later, she's still living at home and is now between jobs.

"We've learned new levels of prayer, praying continually for our granddaughter's protection, that she won't be kidnapped when the dad comes to see her. We pray for her health, her emotional adjustments, and her day-care teachers. We had a baby dedication service with her aunts and uncles standing with her mother and us to promise God we'd all help raise this child in the ways of the Lord. Now four years old, she's remarkably bright and has a spiritual maturity beyond her years.

"Of course we love our daughter and our grandchild and would go to any lengths to help them. But then, we've found ourselves giving up ordinary ways of life, such as no longer inviting our friends over for a late supper because the noise would awaken the baby. The dining room carpet and chairs are stained from food she's spilled. The den has been turned into her play area, and my husband gave up his study so the baby could have a bedroom of her own.

"These sacrifices probably aren't much, but the privacy we miss is something we didn't anticipate. Nor the stress of a little one waking us up at six o'clock in the morning, crying in the middle of the night, or wanting one of us to read one more story or play one more game when we're both exhausted. Life has changed. We have done everything for her that we did for our own four children—from changing diapers, to helping her learn to walk, to teaching her to ride a tricycle. We've helped nurse her through the usual baby health bouts, and we take her on short trips when we can get away for a few days (though she is not a happy camper in a car).

"We found ourselves not only coparenting this precious grandchild but also trying to find help in getting our daughter emotionally healed after she had lived with someone who controlled her every move. When her ex-husband comes to see their daughter, she experiences another setback on her emotional roller coaster. She is a Christian, but sometimes she loses hope of ever being able to live on her own. We've chosen to let her stay as long as necessary—to help her and to provide a Christian atmosphere for our granddaughter. I don't think Jesus would throw someone out on the streets when there is room in your home and heart for a loved one.

"My husband, daughter, and I could not have made it these almost five years had it not been for our prayer partners standing with us. Every time there is a crisis, I pick up the phone and call several friends who will immediately pray us through a situation. God has been faithful in answering our prayers."

Each coparenting situation is different, yet many have some of the same needs:

- A need to forgive those who have wounded your loved one.
- A need to forget the past and move forward with faith that God will see you through.
- A need to pray for finances for life's basics.
- A need to believe that someday this will pass and you will be stronger, more compassionate, and better equipped to help others because of what you've been through, with the help of your all-powerful God.

Raising Your Children's Children

Grandmothers who are raising their grandchildren at a time when they would normally think of retirement are meeting in support groups across the nation in church basements, civic centers, and homes. One woman says her group helps recharge her batteries and offers her encouragement.

The meetings also provide a time for sharing about the red tape and legal headaches sometimes involved in the care of grandkids, as well as a venue for swapping ideas and resources. One grandmom admitted she took on the role of a full-time mom after her daughter became addicted to cocaine and could not be a responsible parent. At first she was ashamed to admit the reason she was raising her grandson, but she found acceptance and security in her support group.

"There are so many of us, and it's just so hard," said one of the group members. "We're all old ladies trying to raise little kids," said another. "Misery loves company, and this kind of normalizes it."[2]

Most of them are quick to say they love their grandchildren but wish they had more stamina, energy, and financial resources. "I don't regret what I'm doing, because I know where my grandchildren are at night—right here with me," one grandmother said.

Many of these children's parents are on drugs or are in prison or have suffered a death in the family that forces grandparents to step in. Some grandmothers in smaller towns say support groups aren't readily available to them, so a few have started their own.[3]

God himself is the one who can help these grandparents get through the years of parenting another little one whether they have a support group or not, as our next story illustrates.

She Adopted Her Grandson

Violet found herself taking care of her little grandson Jerome almost from the moment he was born, since his working parents lived with her and her husband. But Jerome's parents began drifting in and out of the drug scene, and finally, when he was just nine months old, the marriage dissolved. The baby's mother kept him for only three weeks, then left him with Violet.

When Jerome turned two, Violet and her husband, Ernest, went to court to legally adopt him, with both his parents signing their consent. At the time, Violet was forty-nine and Ernest fifty-five, not ages when most people consider starting life over with a toddler to raise. From the time he could talk, Jerome called Violet "Grandmommy" even though she was now officially his mom.

Since they lived out in the country, Jerome had wide open spaces to play in. He followed his beloved granddad around the farm, learning many skills from him. With his grandparents, he attended church regularly, and daily they had family prayers together. As Jerome advanced into his teen years, he began choosing wrong friends and becoming a bit rebellious, although he stayed away from drugs and drinking.

Then, just before Jerome's fifteenth birthday, Ernest died of a heart attack. That blow sent the youngster further into rebellion, and he dropped out of church. He was mad at his granddad for dying, mad at God for taking him, and mad at his parents for deserting him. Furthermore, he rebelled against female authority— primarily his grandmother.

At times he would shout at Violet, and on a few occasions he even shoved her, though she was only about half his size. "I remind you, Lord, he is your child; we dedicated him to you as a baby," she would pray as she cried out to God for help. "I can't handle him, but you can. You have to do something; whatever it takes to bring him back to you, do it."

When Violet decided to sell her house and relocate to a city some sixty miles away, Jerome stubbornly refused to move with her. Finally, the Department of Human Services told him if he didn't move with his grandmother, he'd be considered a runaway. They would pick him up and place him in a home, where he probably wouldn't want to be.

Shocked to learn that his grandmother had such legal recourse, Jerome softened his attitude. He gently asked Violet to consider letting him stay to finish public high school by rooming and boarding with a local family. She agreed.

One night while he was sitting in his car with his girlfriend, playing some loud music, a schoolmate knocked on his car door to tell him to turn it down. When Jerome rolled down the window to talk to him, the young man punched him in the face, broke his nose, and kept on beating him until he could get out of the car and defend himself.

This was a wake-up call for Jerome. He knew if he went to school the next day, this guy would pick a fight and they'd both get expelled. He called Violet to ask if he might enroll in the Christian academy in the town where he was living. For years she had prayed he would want to attend this school, but he never before would consider it. Now she happily agreed and offered to pay the fees.

When Jerome transferred to the Christian school and joined the church youth group, it started him on a journey back to the faith of his grandparents. The following summer, he went to an out-of-state youth camp, where he had a spiritual experience that completely changed his life and his goals.

"He came back changed overnight," Violet said. "He'd always been interested in music, but after that summer camp, he began leading worship in the youth meetings. Attendance rose from twenty-one to seventy in a matter of weeks, and now it's near a hundred. He's not only assistant music director but assistant youth leader as well."

At this writing, Jerome is a straight-A student, is captain of his basketball team, and has earned many school honors, with graduation just months away. His grandmother has been faithful not only to pray but to be there for him at all his school functions. She's always said to him, "I'll never give up on you—and neither will God." And Jerome knows she means it.

"Lots of nights I stay up praying, asking God what to tell him when he's asked for prayer over a difficult predicament," she admitted. "Once, he was forced to cancel his youth band because of complaints its music was not in their denominational hymnals. I prayed with him about the problem, and we both released the situation into God's hands. When the youth attendance plummeted, church leaders asked him to reassemble his band."

No one could be prouder of Jerome than his grandmother. She has helped him get a used car, and she's paid for his room and board and his private school tuition. Now with great faith she prays for his upcoming college tuition, as he'd like to major in music.

Violet has seven other grandchildren, but none of them resent Jerome. They look up to him as their role model since he's the oldest. Jerome has had to come face to face with the fact that he cannot change his parents. His dad, Violet's son, is in jail for forging a drug prescription, but at last he is making a turn toward God.

Recently when Jerome went to visit his mom, she was so high on drugs it was a miserable experience. He called Grandmother Violet at 3:30 in the morning, sobbing with grief. Then he drove to her house and they stayed up the rest of the night talking. Violet read him Scriptures about the need for him to forgive his mom. Slowly he's working through that process, and he now realizes the only thing he can do for his birth parents is to pray for them.

Violet advises other grandparents to stand in the prayer gap for their grandchildren. "God didn't give up on King David when he made mistakes, and we can't give up either," she said. "As a widow, it was hard for me to handle Jerome, but I knew the mighty power of the God I serve. It took patience, and I am not a patient person. But God has helped both of us to change."

Jerome is one happy and blessed grandchild. And he loves Grandmother Violet all the more for the sacrifices she's made for him.

Learning to Let Go

Florence is a grandmother who suffered the pain of becoming a substitute parent to her grandchildren, only to have them taken from her and given up for adoption. Yet her relationship with God was deepened through the ordeal.

"Although we raised our children to know and love the Lord, our daughter, Miriam, became pregnant when she was fifteen. She carried the baby full term but often talked about giving it up for adoption. I told her I would support her decision but warned her that if she brought the baby home, I would be too attached to part with it later on.

"She did bring home a sweet, tiny five-pound girl she named Suzanne. I was hopelessly in love with her from the moment I saw her. Miriam had already quit school during the pregnancy, and because she was nursing the baby, she couldn't go back. But after three months, she decided she didn't want to be a mother. One day she just left home, leaving the baby behind.

"At first I was in shock, but in a way, I was relieved. Sometimes Miriam had been careless with the baby and would get angry when Suzanne awakened her at night. I slept lightly and always heard the baby cry. I'd get up and take Suzanne to Miriam for nursing, wait for her to finish, then take the baby back to her crib.

"After Miriam left, I got Suzanne on a routine of feeding, playing, waking, and sleeping. I took her everywhere with me and enjoyed watching her learn about everything—birds, grass, flowers, dogs. We laughed, sang, and played together for two years. She brought a long-needed joy into my life, and of course, I prayed for her daily.

"Then Miriam had a second child—a plump, happy boy—and moved back home. I followed the same routine as before. I would awaken when the baby cried and get up at night to care for his needs. I fell in love with him, too.

"Miriam then married the father of her son. She and the children continued to live with us, but her husband visited only occasionally. When my grandson was four months old, they decided to move out of state and take both the children with them. Of course I wanted them to get their life together, but it was torture to part with the children. The day they left, I cried all day while praying that God would keep them safe.

"Although we tried to phone them regularly, it became harder and harder to catch them at home. Then one day we got the awful news! Our son called to tell us that Miriam had given the children up for adoption as soon as they'd arrived at their new place.

"When I heard that, I burst into tears, ran into the bathroom, and threw up. I felt as if a part of me had been torn away. My heart ached. My body ached. How could she give up the babies I loved so dearly? Why didn't she just leave them with us? They were ours . . . they were mine. I grieved as though they were dead.

"My husband flew into action. He called a lawyer, who advised us to get a lawyer in the state where they had moved. It took days of contacting several agencies, going through a child-find group, and spending lots of money. We learned that, legally, we probably didn't have a chance to get them back, but we wanted to keep trying.

"One day as I poured out my heart to God, begging him to return the children, he made it clear that I had not asked what he wanted for them. I then prayed, 'Lord, make my will your will.' A great peace came over me, and I knew he wanted us to let the children go. I didn't understand it at all, but I yielded. I had felt such hatred toward Miriam, but now those feelings began to fade into sorrow for her. It seemed she had given up everything, including her children, parents, and siblings. But now, for the first time, a hope began to grow in my heart. Somehow I knew the children were in God's care.

"Then the Lord led me to call our daughter and tell her I loved her no matter what. My hatred and sorrow were replaced with compassion. When Miriam asked me to forgive her, and I told her I did, it lifted a huge burden off both of us.

"She explained that she had given up the children because she wanted them to have a mom and dad who could meet their needs—emotionally, physically, and spiritually. If my husband and I were to raise her children, she would always feel guilty, perhaps even resent us for putting them ahead of her.

"I still miss my grandchildren. I cry, ache to hold them, and long to hear their sweet voices—especially on their birthdays and at Christmas. Walking through a store and seeing children's clothes and toys brings me to tears. But God has taught me about putting others' needs ahead of mine in such a deep way that I am changed because of going through this loss. I know the children are in a Christian home, and they're an answer to prayer for a couple who trusted God for ten years to adopt one child. Now they have two.

"The adoptive parents send us pictures and letters about our grandchildren. In turn, we send pictures, letters, and gifts to them. I've learned to live in a place of trust in my heavenly Father that I never knew before. He is able to turn sorrow into gladness and give me joy for mourning.

"Many friends have told me that they would never have given up trying to get their grandchildren back. Normally, I would agree with them. But now I know how wonderful it is to walk in the peace that comes from yielding to the all-wise God. He is restoring my relationship with my daughter in a loving way. As we learn to trust each other, I see her through God's eyes more each day."[4]

Granddad Grateful for Godly Example

Grandparents who now find themselves as full-time caregivers to grandchildren may feel overwhelmed by the task. But if they are blessed to have happy childhood memories of times spent in their own grandparents' home, they can put into practice the wholesome things they experienced there.

Grandfather George, who is now raising his fourteen-year-old granddaughter, believes his grandparents' example to him when he was young has enhanced his ability to share family values with his grandchild.

"Had it not been for my dear grandparents, I probably wouldn't have such a positive influence in her life today," George said. "They were simple, country people who spent their entire lives on a farm, without any formal education or training in how to raise kids. Yet their love and affection contributed greatly to creating the better side of me. They had a natural ability to show love to all their grandchildren. I pray that the heritage which fell to me will be passed on to my grandchildren and to generations to come."

Remembering Nana

Betty, a successful businesswoman, pays tribute to the grandmother who became a surrogate mother to her. After her parents divorced when she was ten, Betty and her younger brother went to live with Nana.

"From the time we started living with her until both of us graduated from college, Nana provided a loving home for us and trained us up in the way she thought we should go," Betty said. "A big part of that training was our spiritual development. There was no question in our house about where you would be on Sunday mornings. Sunday school and church were the order of the day. Her rule was that if you didn't feel well enough to go to church in the morning, then everything else was out for that day."

Through Nana's example, Betty and her brother learned the importance of living your faith every day, not just at church, where Nana served in several capacities. Nana believed in helping others, and Betty delivered many a meal to neighbors. Although she had meager means herself, Nana always was eager to share what she had with those in need.

"Every morning, she would pull back the kitchen curtain to welcome the day," Betty said. "I always heard her say, 'Father, I stretch my hand to you; no other help I know. If thou withdraw thyself from me, Lord, where would I go?'"

Nana had learned early in life to depend on God for everything. Raised by her grandmother after her mother died at a young age, Nana married at age fourteen and was widowed twice by the time she was in her early thirties. Left with six children to care for, she went to work as a maid.

"She managed, with meager resources, to provide a home and a good solid upbringing for her kids," Betty said. "But then she helped to raise us grandkids as well. She was an inspiration to me as I pursued my studies and was a key contributor to my academic success and to my obtaining scholarships for college. I thank God for her and for her influence on the person that I am today. She still lives on in me and in my children as I've tried to pass on to my sons the love of God, the love of people, and the many pearls of wisdom that she gave me."

As we've seen in this chapter, when grandparents take on the role of parent or coparent, there are numerous challenges yet many dividends. It may take years before the efforts of a godly, praying grandparent are appreciated by the child he or she helped to raise. But God knows. He sees. He helps. And he rewards.

One of those rewards, Grandmother, is to realize that you are leaving a lasting legacy for your grandchild, as Nana did for Betty.

Prayer

Lord, I ask you to provide all I'll need in helping to raise my grandchildren at such a critical time in their lives. Please give me stamina, patience, wisdom, finances, and a sense of humor. Show me how to discipline them in a just and fair manner. Most of all, let me express unconditional love to them, so that through me they will know your love for them. Be with their parents, who may be feeling guilty because I'm now primary caregiver for their children. Show them when and how to respond to these children who are missing them. Thank you that you care so much for families. I want to do my part to keep ours together. Help me, Lord, to accomplish that. I thank you in advance for equipping and enabling me for this new role. Amen.

Helpful Scriptures

If the LORD delights in a man's way,
    he makes his steps firm;
though he stumble, he will not fall,
    for the LORD upholds him with his hand.
I was young and now I am old,
    yet I have never seen the righteous forsaken
    or their children begging bread.
They are always generous and lend freely;
    their children will be blessed.

—Psalm 37:23–26

Let your conversation be always full of grace, seasoned with salt, so that you may know how to answer everyone.

—Colossians 4:6

Devote yourselves to prayer, being watchful and thankful.

—Colossians 4:2

Scripture Prayer

Lord, please help me to be devoted to my grandchild [name] with genuine affection, and to take delight in honoring [him/her]. Help me not to be lazy in my work, but to serve you enthusiastically. Help me to be glad for all you are planning for me and for [name] and to be patient in trouble and always prayerful [Rom. 12:10–12 NLT].

Related Scripture References

Psalms 10:12–14; 27:13–14; 68:5–6
1 Corinthians 15:58
Philippians 4:12–13
James 1:27

Leaving a Lasting Legacy

O God, you have helped me from my earliest child-hood—and I have constantly testified to others of the wonderful things you do. And now that I am old and gray, don't forsake me. Give me time to tell this new generation (and their children too) about all your mighty miracles.

—Psalm 71:17–18 TLB

Have you given yourself and your family a sense of value in the grand march of eternity? A sense of worth and well-being that there is no other family in the entire world exactly like yours? Have you made them aware of their unique place and time in history?

—JoAn Summers, *Keepers of the Treasure*

Grandparents often fulfill the important role of providing stability and moral support to families. They leave a legacy, a bequest of something valuable from the past. As Christians, what we hope to leave is a spiritual legacy.

I (Quin) saw an example of this one February evening some ten years ago when I attended the memorial service for noted

Christian author and pastor Jamie Buckingham, who was my friend and mentor. With Jackie, his widow, standing at the front surrounded by their five children and thirteen grandchildren, one of the pastors made a surprising announcement.

"We are here to commemorate the life of a special friend, father, and pastor," he said. "But today also is a time to pass on the family legacy to the next generation. Moses is dead, but Joshua will inherit the Promised Land."

Then Jamie's son, Tim, held his infant son, Joshua Buckingham, while the pastor led in prayer to dedicate this newest grandchild to the Lord. My eyes focused on Jackie, who stood next to Tim, smiling and patting the baby. I knew she was adding her prayers to those of the pastor and family members gathered around her.

Jamie had been buried privately by his family a few days earlier; this memorial service was for friends to celebrate his homegoing. Christian leaders had flown into Melbourne, Florida, from around the world to honor one of Christendom's most prolific writers. After several of them had given short eulogies, we were in for another surprise. Jamie's last will and testament was read aloud to the congregation, recounting the Christian heritage passed to him from his parents, followed by an account of his experience with the Lord. It ended by challenging his offspring to continue passing on their spiritual heritage from generation to generation.

I listened, enthralled, trying to imagine how his children and grandchildren must have felt to hear these words as they were saying their good-byes to the family patriarch. Jamie's message assured them that he was already in heaven with his Lord and that because of their choice to follow Jesus, they would see him again someday.

Examples in Prayer

Jamie and Jackie were devoted, praying grandparents. At one time, all five of their children lived on the tree-studded property surrounding the "big house," appropriately named Hebron—the name for a city of refuge in the Bible. Laughter and noisy conversation echoed from the family homestead as cousins swam in the pool and popped in and out to see their grandparents. Today only three of the children with their families reside on the site, but it is still a lively place. Jackie now carries the responsibility of praying faithfully for her fourteen grandchildren.

"I pray for their protection and ask God to pave the way for his kingdom to come in each one of their lives," she said. "I ask him to remove obstacles that keep them from seeking God's best and doing it. Mainly, I pray for their parents to make wise decisions in rearing these children. Every day I pray differently, but I cover all of them in prayer daily."

As Jackie's example illustrates, our prayer strategies need to change as our grandchildren's needs change. For instance, one daughter recently moved to another state when her husband got a job transfer, so Jackie now prays "long distance" for those four grandchildren.

Creating a Legacy

Grandmothers, like Lois in the Bible (see 2 Tim. 1:5), can serve as spiritual models for their grandchildren as they daily demonstrate the reality of walking with God through good as well as tough times. Whether we're aware of it or not, we are continually in the process of creating a legacy that will be passed on to our grandchildren and the generations to follow.

Nell told us of her childhood memories of visiting her grandmother's home and learning the importance of prayer. "When I'd sleep over at her house, the first thing we did after getting up in the morning was to pray," she said. "And praying was the last thing we did at night, as well as at every meal. My grandmother was the only person I've ever known who had calluses on her knees from praying; for her, praying was as natural as breathing. She often took me and my cousins on long walks in the woods to visit a little creek where we went wading, and she taught us how to make hats and boats out of leaves and twigs. I will never forget how special it was to kneel outside beside the creek with the breeze in our faces as she taught us how to pray. What a wonderful heritage!"

Today Nell is passing that heritage on to her son and grandchildren, as well as to the many students she has influenced in her years of teaching. She now heads up the Christian education department of a large university where she is training future teachers, instilling in them an appreciation for the value of prayer.

Barbara, a grandmother of five, says she has prayed more for her grandchildren than she did for her children because she now better understands the power of prayer. But she also prays for nations around the world. In the past fifteen years, she has traveled to six continents on prayer missions. She credits her maternal grandmother, whom she calls Nana, as having the dominant spiritual influence on her growing up years.

Since her mother was continually in and out of psychiatric hospitals, Barbara and her only sister spent nine summers with Nana in Oklahoma. For them this was home and their favorite place to be, though it was only a small four-room farmhouse with no running water, electricity, or indoor bathroom. Though Nana was poor, her grandchildren didn't know it. She taught her granddaughters how to tend a garden as she raised her own fruits and vegetables and shared the bounty with neighbors. Barbara's summers spent with Nana taught her the principles of plowing, sowing, weeding, and harvesting. Good lessons to learn, both physically and spiritually.

Nana taught her granddaughters the fear of the Lord and that church is a place to reverence God. Every morning, she attended Mass, and that meant Barbara and her sister went, too. It was just natural to start off your day talking to God.

"Though I didn't have a mother to love and comfort me, Nana was my excellent substitute," Barbara said. "I always knew she was there for me. She kept a threadbare rug next to her bed where she knelt to pray every morning and evening. I would listen and marvel at her prayers. I'm sure my family will never know, in this life, the full effect of them."

Blessing the Younger Generation

Now Barbara passes on this legacy to her grandchildren. Once when she was visiting her son's home, her oldest grandson, Stephen, came into the kitchen where she was and gave her a big bear hug. As he pulled away, she suddenly said, "Stephen, could I pray for you? I believe God wants to release a blessing into your life from your grandmother."

"Sure, Gram," he responded.

Barbara prayed for God's divine purpose and blessing to be released into his life, and she prayed over the college he was planning to attend the next year. "When I prayed over his choice of a life mate and thanked God for already having her picked out for him, I heard Stephen chuckle," she said. "But I just kept on praying. Then my husband joined me and pronounced a grandfather's blessing over his life."

Some time later, Stephen wrote this about his grandmother: "I always have the comfort of knowing that Gram is blanketing me with prayers and that God is watching over my life. I feel God has always been with me and kept me safe, and I owe a lot of that to my grandmother. I've been able to stay out of trouble in this horrible world because of her prayers and the Lord's intervention in my life. I thank God for her every day."

Many Grandparents, Different Expressions

Amy grew up with seven grandparents who influenced her life in various ways. The fact that all were wonderful Christians with different expressions of faith helped her immensely. "I thought everyone had opportunity to learn from several grandparents," she said. "But in talking to my friends, I found not only that they did not have as many as I did but that not all of them had Christian grandparents. Then I really began to appreciate my blessings."

Three grandmothers in particular had an important spiritual impact on Amy, one of whom was her great-grandmother, Dale Evans Rogers. Amy refers to her as "Gigi," for great-grandmother.

"I always was safe unburdening my heart to Grandma Gigi, and she never criticized me," Amy said. "She'd give me advice if I asked, but she never was negative. She had lived two different lives—one as a nonbeliever, and then after her son, Tom, led her to the Lord, she became this amazing Christian. Her commitment to the Lord was incredible. She was so wise but so full of fun; I had the highest respect for her. Integrity is the word I think of when remembering her. She never missed a day praying for her children, grandchildren, and great-grandchildren, each one by name."

Once when Amy made a difficult decision that meant ending a friendship, Grandma Gigi was her biggest supporter. "When it seems you have lost everything, just remember that you haven't," Grandma Gigi said. "That just wasn't the Lord's best for you. I am behind your decision and am so proud of you for making it."

From her Grandmother Petersen, Amy learned the importance of consistency and how discipline pays off. This grandmother spent a good many years as a dorm mother at a school in Japan where she was mother to many youngsters. "She reads her Bible faithfully, is very sincere, and has an unswerving Christian life," Amy said. "While she has only three grandchildren, she prays daily for them. I love her dearly."

Of her Grandmother Fox, she said, "Nana is so self-sacrificing. She would lay down her life for any of us in the family, and every single day, she prays for her eight grandchildren. I grow to love and respect her more each time we have contact. The fact that all three of my grandmothers were so different from one another has helped me be a better Christian by observing their lifestyles."

Dale Evans was thirty-five when she returned to the precepts of her Christian mother's teaching, which she had learned at the feet of her grandparents. She tells about one of her forefathers who was jailed for preaching the gospel on the streets instead of adhering to the dictates of the Church of England. But jail didn't stop him from preaching from the window of his cell to the people down below.

"His genes are strong in me," Dale wrote. "Since making Jesus Christ my Lord as well as Savior, I believe his heritage is partly responsible for my forthright declaration of Christian faith in the midst of a show business career, even at the expense of a contract. The Lord has told us to build our homes on solid rock. . . . If we have a spiritual heritage, we have a firm foundation to withstand the turmoil around us. We won't be blown away when the storms break loose . . . as they will."[1]

Passing It On

Billy and Ruth Graham's daughter, Gigi, is the eldest of five children who grew up in their North Carolina mountain home. She remembers the godly influence of her maternal grandparents, who lived nearby. There she and her siblings spent many pleasant days. She felt free to run over a little stream and down a lane to the back door of her grandparents' house, which was never locked. As retired missionaries who had ministered for many years in China, they made it a priority to be there to help Ruth Graham raise her children. "I struggle to express how grateful I am for the influence my grandparents had on my values and character," Gigi wrote years later when she herself was a mother of seven and grandmother of fifteen.[2]

She still remembers nights spent at her maternal grandparents' home. In the early morning, she'd wake up in the small upstairs sleeping porch and savor the aroma of bacon, eggs, and hot biscuits drifting up from her grandmother's kitchen. On her way downstairs, she would pass the corner of the living room, where she could always see Grandfather Bell on his knees in front of the big rocking chair, praying.[3]

The other Graham grandparents lived in a red brick farmhouse on a small dairy farm just two hours away, where Gigi and her siblings enjoyed visiting as they grew up. On her final visit to Mother Graham's farmhouse with her own children, Gigi went with a heavy heart, knowing it would be her last good-bye.

But the frail, white-haired grandmother was radiant with joy at seeing her grandchildren and great-grandchildren. One by one they approached her bedside. She took each one in her feeble arms, repeating a special Scripture verse or blessing over them, and in a weak voice added, "Pass it on." A few days later, she died. Thus Billy Graham's mom left a spiritual heritage to all those in her lineage, a spiritual inheritance that outlives her.[4]

I (Ruthanne) have two stepdaughters whose grandparents on both sides of the family left them a wonderful legacy of faith in God. Melody, the younger daughter, shares her memories of her two grandmothers.

A Symbol of Love

"One of my earliest childhood memories is receiving a birthday card from my Grandma Rains with a one-dollar bill in it. Since I was living in South Africa at the time and had left the United States at the age of six months, I couldn't remember ever even meeting this distant grandmother. But I do remember understanding that the woman who sent it seemed to know me and care about me and expressed her affection in the only way she knew how.

"She occasionally sent me cash or even larger checks throughout the rest of her life until she entered a nursing home. Whether it was for birthdays or Christmas, college expenses or other needs, I knew the money was only a symbol of her love and prayers for me.

"When my parents returned from their missions assignment in South Africa, our family lived in the basement of Grandma Rains' house during part of my first-grade year. Every morning after breakfast, Grandma could be found in her special chair, reading Scripture and praying. We all knew the rest of the day could not proceed until she'd had her prayer time and Bible reading. As a kid, I didn't think much of her prayer sessions, but later, I came to realize that I benefited greatly from her prayers.

"After my mother died when I was seven years old, my dad took my sister and me on many weekend trips to Kansas to visit Grandma Rains as well as Aunt Eileen, who became almost a surrogate mother for us during that year. It was a safe place that seemed like a haven of stability in our upside-down world and a place where we knew we were loved.

"To me, Grandma Rains always represented integrity. When Grandpa's business thrived and he wanted to build her a new house, she insisted that they first give generously to the new church building. 'God's house first, then ours,' she told him. Forty years later, that small congregation still enjoys the benefits of Grandma's clear priorities.

"For years, even when she couldn't attend, she insisted that the church women's group meet in her home for their weekly Bible study, and she regularly housed visiting preachers and missionaries. Somehow she managed to give away any extras to family members or friends. When she had to move into a nursing facility and it came time to clean out her house, there was remarkably little stuff to deal with.

"Now, when I'm struggling to find a balance between the demands of family, church, and job, memories of Grandma Rains come drifting back. Remembering her example helps me focus on the real priorities. Whether I have little or much doesn't really matter, as long as it is all surrendered to the Lord."

Obstacles Didn't Stop Her

"Grandma Garlock, on the other hand, who, with Grandpa, did pioneer missions work in Africa in the early 1920s, was the heroine of all my favorite missionary stories. To me she represented the idea that you can do anything you set your mind to, provided God's in it. Once she was clear on what God was calling her to do, she knew it was going to happen; the how of the matter was incidental.

"Visits from Grandma and the stories I heard about her made a lasting impression. Ruth Eveline Garlock started out a simple New Jersey schoolteacher but became a missionary to Africa working in areas where no white person had ever gone. Returning to Africa with her husband and two children in 1932, she helped to create an alphabet and translate the Bible into the language of the Dagombas, a tribe in northern Ghana.

"Grandma Garlock could speak multiple African dialects, administrate the affairs of a remote mission station, earn the respect of local African tribespeople, homeschool her children, laugh more heartily than anyone I ever knew, sew anything, cook anything—with only one pot—and can apricots (or anything else from Grandpa's garden) by the ton. She could preach up a storm, survive numerous bouts of tropical fevers, inspire young people to become missionaries, sing with gusto an octave lower than all the other women, intercede in prayer for hours, and teach the Bible so you'd never forget it.

"Never one to be intimidated by obstacles, she simply followed God's leading throughout her ninety-nine years of life. Now, when I feel frustrated about homeschooling my children and think I can't do it anymore, I can almost hear Grandma reminding me that God can.

"Other significant legacies she left me are her prayer life and study of the Bible. In their retirement years, both my grandparents were known for their prayer book—a simple notebook containing prayer requests they prayed over every day. All their children and grandchildren were listed, along with specific needs. Friends, pastors, missionaries, ministries, and government leaders also were included. Getting one's name into that book was a coveted privilege! I'm convinced that many of the blessings in my life today are the result of my grandparents' years of unrelenting prayer for me.

"I am blessed to own one of Grandma Garlock's many well-marked Bibles. It is frayed, stained, and underlined, but I enjoy studying the verses that were especially meaningful to her, along with her marginal notes. God was real and powerful in her life because she immersed herself in his Word, and God's promises strengthened and sustained her. I sometimes ask myself, How can I be so casual about it?

"My rich spiritual heritage is a wonderful blessing, though the example set by my grandmothers is hard to live up to. But because they were real women whom I knew and loved—not storybook characters—I realize that if God could work in their lives, he can work in mine, too. I pray that I will be able to pass on this legacy to my own children and grandchildren."

Four Generations Enjoy One Another

When Mitzi's mom and dad, both in their eighties, came to live near her, God gave the elderly couple a fresh outlook on life. Now, every Sunday, four generations get together to eat after church, either in a restaurant or in one of their homes. When the group is in public, people smile as the great-grandkids run to embrace Nana and Papa and as the extended family bows for a blessing on the meal.

"Having their grandparents and great-grandparents close by means my sons have six adults to let them know how absolutely awesome they are," says Mitzi's daughter, Roberta, mother of four young sons. "And they offer loving guidance when the kids *aren't* so awesome. All four grandparents know firsthand the prayer needs of my sons, but they also know where the diapers and wipes are at my house. My boys never need wonder what Grandma or Grandpa or Nana and Papa look like. To them, Grandma is a real person who gives warm kisses and loving hugs and does a great Donald Duck impression. Sometimes when I'm too tired to laugh at their jokes, Grandma isn't.

"I need my folks and my grandparents and am daily thankful they are close enough to touch. My sons have learned to sing 'Have You Ever Gone A-Fishing?' while dancing around Great-Grandaddy (Papa) as he strums his guitar, just as I once did, and my mom before me. What a legacy we have."

One grandmother throws a party on the birthday of her deceased mom. She invites all her grandchildren, then she and their parents tell stories about the life of their godly matriarch. Thus the great-grandchildren can feel they know her, too.

A Grandmother's Gifts

I (Quin) shared in chapter 3 about my mother's relationship with my children. My daughter, Quinett, the oldest granddaughter in the family, feels her grandmother imparted two distinct gifts to her.

"One gift Mother Jewett imparted to me was the gift of hospitality. She was always feeding a crowd, and not just the Sunday family lunch. Because she cared for people, she drew them around her table for any occasion—birthdays, milestones, or to honor a special event. She knew that a table of food brought people together. Around the table, relationships with others could be cemented.

"Since our Lord is a relationship God, all our friendships and families grow out of this covenant of connecting. And Mother Jewett knew how to help that happen. She cared enough to teach me not just how to cook but how to enjoy what I cook with family, friends, and all who would visit our home. This gift of hospitality is now being passed on to the fourth generation—my own children—as I try to foster these qualities in them.

"The second gift I received from her is the gift of praise and worship. Although she didn't have a professional singer's voice, my grandmother always had little praise choruses she would sing aloud. One Christmas, when I was about eight, she gave me a box of rhythm band instruments. At first I thought the gift should have been for a younger child. But my siblings and I used those instruments when we had times of worship with my parents in our home. We all especially liked the tambourine, and later, when we went to Bible school, my sister and I learned how to play it.

"Now my own children play these same instruments, here in our home and at Mama Quin's. The significance of the tambourine for me is that my grandmother knew something about praise and worship and touching heaven's throne, and she imparted that to me.

"I named my daughter Victoria Jewett so that these same gifts of hospitality and worship would continue to be passed down to the next generation. I know that Mother Jewett is in heaven cheering all of us on to finish the race on earth and bring glory to the Lord."

A Relay Race

Author Edith Schaeffer describes a family as a perpetual relay of truth. She writes, "I think we can see the whole race as one in which true truth is to be handed over like the flag in a relay race. We are responsible for 'handing on the flag' and for being very careful not to drop it—or to drop out—because of our responsibility to the next generation. . . . If those who knew God and who had so very much to tell about Him had always been faithful, and had always stuck to . . . the rules of the relay, there would have been no gaps. Each generation would have learned from the one before. Fathers and mothers were to tell sons and daughters. There was supposed to be a perpetual relay of truth without a break."[5]

We want to do our part to carry the flag in this race for our family's future, and we hope you share this desire. May each of us determine to leave a lasting legacy to our children's children, one that will continue for generations to come—a legacy of love, spiritual influence, and prayer.

Prayer

Lord, how I thank you for the opportunity to sow prayers into my grandchildren's future. I pray that not one of those prayers will go unanswered. But you will answer them in your timing and in your most perfect way. I trust you, Lord, with my grandchildren and their children after them. Thank you for the opportunity I've had to pray for them through hard times and good times. Bless them with your abundant love. I praise you for these grandchildren who have enriched my life and made it full. Amen.

Helpful Scriptures

Only be careful, and watch yourselves closely so that you do not forget the things your eyes have seen or let them slip from your heart as long as you live. Teach them to your children and to their children after them.

—Deuteronomy 4:9

The LORD is the portion of my inheritance and my cup;
    Thou dost support my lot.
The lines have fallen to me in pleasant places;
    Indeed, my heritage is beautiful to me.

—Psalm 16:5–6 NASB

I will open my mouth in parables,
    I will utter hidden things, things from of old—
what we have heard and known,
    what our fathers have told us.
We will not hide them from their children;
    we will tell the next generation
the praiseworthy deeds of the LORD,
    his power, and the wonders he has done.

—Psalm 78:2–4

Scripture Prayer

Lord, I pray that my grandchildren [names] will throw off everything that hinders them and the sin that so easily entangles. May they run with perseverance the race marked out for them. Let them fix their eyes on Jesus, the author and perfecter of their faith, who for the joy set before him endured the cross, scorning its shame, and sat down at the right hand of the throne of God [Heb. 12:1–2].

Related Scripture References

Psalms 119:111; 127:3–5
Isaiah 54:17; 61:8–9
Matthew 25:34
2 Timothy 1:5

Epilogue

When we think of godly influence in a family, the norm usually is for the older ones to pass on their spiritual heritage to the younger ones. But in some cases, it's the young who influence their elders. My hairdresser recently told me about an experience she had when her two three-year-old granddaughters spent the night with her.

"The next morning we were sitting out on the patio as they ate their cereal at a little picnic table," she said. "I was in a lounge chair with my feet up when a bee landed on my ankle and stung me. Since I'm allergic to bee stings, my first thought was to rush to the doctor's office. 'See this red spot on Honey's ankle?' I said to the girls. 'That's where a bee stung me, and in a few minutes my foot will be all sore and swollen. I'm going to have to call your mothers to come pick you up right away so I can go to the doctor.'"

The two cousins ran over to their grandmother's chair to examine the spot. "No, Honey, no," Alex declared insistently, shaking her head. "We'll pray for you, and Jesus will heal you!"

"They put their hands on my ankle, bowed their little heads and prayed a simple prayer, asking Jesus to heal my bee sting," Honey said. "When they took their hands away, the spot was gone, and the swelling I'd expected never happened. Instead, the three of us had a fun day together. I had been teaching them that Jesus hears and answers our prayers, but I was humbled by their simple, childlike faith."

Anna, a young Chinese friend of mine, was the first in her devoutly Buddhist family to become a Christian. She married into a Christian family, and she and her husband, Victor, attended the denominational church in which he had grown up. More than ten years passed before they finally had a child—a son they named Timothy, who immediately became the delight of the entire family, especially Anna's elderly mother.

For years Victor and Anna had prayed that her parents would accept Christ, and they had tried to witness to them. But the parents were fiercely loyal to the religious traditions of their ancestors. Although they had gone to Victor and Anna's church for special occasions, they were not comfortable with attending services in a typical church building where a cross was displayed.

"After Timothy's birth, my parents started visiting us on weekends, and Mom would even stay over at our place," Anna said. "When she told me she longed to have more time with her new grandson, the Lord gave me an idea. If instead of going to our denominational church, we started attending a Christian fellowship which meets in a hotel ballroom, perhaps Mom would be willing to come along. Sure enough, she agreed to go, and Dad didn't oppose her."

When Anna would take Timothy to the hotel room that was set up as a baby nursery, the grandmother would stay with him. But the young ladies working in the nursery were trained to do more than just take care of the babies and toddlers. They told Bible stories about Jesus and his love and taught the toddlers to sing simple gospel songs. Soon the grandmother was listening to the stories and learning the songs, then singing them to Timothy.

"When Mom had to have a minor operation to remove a small growth on her neck, I asked the three nursery workers to pray for her," Anna said. "The following Sunday, one of the workers told Mom they would be praying for her as she went to the hospital. Then she asked if Mom would like to invite Jesus into her heart."

The young lady's loving manner and simple presentation of the gospel touched the Buddhist grandmother's heart, and she repeated a prayer asking Jesus to become Lord of her life. Two days later, doctors discovered that Anna's mother had a rapidly advancing form of cancer, and the treatments they tried over the following weeks were ineffective. Her days were numbered, but she continued attending worship services with Anna and Victor and spent as much time as possible with her beloved grandson.

During the final few days of her life, one of Anna's brothers offered to bring a minister to the hospice to pray for their mother and administer baptism. "My brother is not a Christian, but he had heard of healing miracles in the church, and his love for Mom moved him to seek help from a minister," Anna told me. "Even though she wasn't healed, my brother knew it would mean a lot to Mom to receive Christian baptism."

When members of the extended family came to the wake, they were surprised to see it was a Christian funeral. Many asked, "Was your mother baptized?" since to a Buddhist, baptism is considered a sure sign that the person is a Christian. Anna and all her brothers and sisters-in-law were very pleased to be able to say, "Yes, Mom was baptized."

A few weeks after the funeral, Anna received a phone call from a cousin who related a dream she'd had. "In my dream, a group of us, including your mom, were on a tour together, and the itinerary included a visit to a Chinese temple," the woman said. "When we went into the temple, I tried to give your mom some jos sticks to burn, knowing she had always offered prayers when visiting a temple. But this time she said, 'No, I don't want them because I've accepted Jesus Christ as my Lord.'"

What a comfort to Anna to realize that her mother is with the Lord and that her own little Timothy had been the instrument God used to lead his grandmother to Jesus.

The reality is that we can encourage our grandchildren through our love, our prayers, and our example. But the blessings go full circle and return to enrich our own lives beyond measure.

—Ruthanne Garlock

Appendix

Hindrances to Prayer

While we yearn to have our prayers answered, a close study of God's Word tells us he has some conditions for answering our prayers. Three of the greatest hindrances to answered prayer are unbelief, unforgiveness, and unconfessed sin.

Jesus addresses the first two in Mark 11:24–25: "Therefore I tell you, whatever you ask for in prayer, believe that you have received it, and it will be yours. And when you stand praying, if you hold anything against anyone, forgive him, so that your Father in heaven may forgive you your sins." It is a twofold condition: to believe that God hears and then to forgive.

He also encourages us to get our hearts right before him. "If we confess our sins, he is faithful and just and will forgive us our sins and purify us from all unrighteousness" (1 John 1:9).

At the beginning of any prayer time, it is helpful to confess any unforgiveness, judgmental attitude, hatred, disappointment, unbelief, or anything that is displeasing to God. With the lines of our communication with the Father open, we can expect to receive an answer to our prayer.

Suggested Service for a Baby Dedication

Following is the order of service Quin's husband, LeRoy, used for the dedication of their newest grandchild, conducted at the home of Ethan's parents.

Father, we have gathered as family members to present and dedicate to you Ethan Keil Sherrer. We thank you for your presence in our hearts. We acknowledge that you knew Ethan even before he was formed, and we have assembled to pronounce a blessing upon him.

We read in Isaiah 44:3, "I will pour out my Spirit on your offspring, and my blessing on your descendants." Today we stand on that promise that God will pour out his blessing on Ethan. Keith and Dana, you are coming to dedicate Ethan Kiel to the Lord, as witnessed by our family gathered around you. I want to ask you to reaffirm your faith.

Do you acknowledge Jesus as your Lord and Savior?
Answer: We do.

Do you promise to raise Ethan in the nurture and admonition of the Lord?
Answer: We do.

We come to present and dedicate Ethan, asking that "the Spirit of the LORD will rest on him—the Spirit of wisdom and of understanding, the Spirit of counsel and of power, the Spirit of knowledge and of the fear of the LORD" (Isa. 11:2).

Let us pray: Heavenly Father, we ask you to send angels to protect Ethan and for the Holy Spirit to teach and guide him. May Jesus always be his best friend. May he, like Jesus, increase "in wisdom and stature, and in favor with God and men" (Luke 2:52). May your kingdom come, your will be done in his life, Lord. Amen.

Do family members gathered here promise to help Ethan to grow up in a Christian environment?
Answer: We will, with God's help.

Ethan, I anoint you with oil in the name of the Father, the Son, and the Holy Spirit and ask God's richest blessings on you all the days of your life.

LeRoy takes Ethan from Keith, then lifts him up to God, saying:
"The LORD will keep you from all harm—he will watch over your life; the LORD will watch over your coming and going both now and forevermore" (Ps. 121:7–8).

"The LORD bless you and keep you; the LORD make his face shine upon you and be gracious to you; the LORD turn his face toward you and give you peace" (Num. 6:24–26).

Lord, we thank you for this precious child. Keep him strong and healthy that he may fulfill your purposes in his life. We seal this blessing in the name of the Father, the Son, and the Holy Spirit. Amen!

Grandparents and Parents in Agreement

My son, Keith, and his wife, Dana, pray with great fervor for their three small children. One day my daughter-in-law brought me these prayers to pray in agreement with her and my son:

- That they will have the unfading beauty of a gentle and quiet spirit (1 Peter 3:4).
- That they will have cheerfully obedient spirits (Eph. 6:1–2).
- That the Lord will protect them—body, soul, spirit— against danger, harm, and evil (1 Thess. 5:23; Ps. 91:14).
- That they will be filled with the fruits of the Spirit (Gal. 5:22–24).
- That they will known Jesus is their best friend and that they can tell him everything.
- That they will fall in love with the Lord and enjoy him, and in turn lead many to love him.
- That they will know Mommy and Daddy love and accept them no matter what they do.
- We claim their lives for salvation and redemption.
- We pray they will have discernment and wisdom to choose the paths of righteousness.
- We pray they will influence others for good and for God wherever they go.
- We pray that, in every season of their lives, the Lord will give them godly friends who will encourage them in the Lord.

- We pray Psalm 121, that the Lord will be their keeper.
- We pray that they will know early in life God's purpose for their future and that as parents and grandparents we will nurture that purpose and their giftings with wisdom.
- We pray that the Lord will keep them and their future spouses for each other and that their spouses will be raised in godly homes and choose righteous paths.[1]

Sample Prayer Journal Page

Child's name: _____.

Thank you, Lord, that you know the plans you have for [name] to prosper and not harm [him/her], but to give [him/her] hope and a future. I pray that my grandchild will not stand in the way of sinners or sit in the seat of mockers. May [his/her] delight be in the law of the Lord as [he/she] meditates on it day and night [Jer. 29:11; Ps. 1:1–2].

Father, may [name], like your Son Jesus, grow in wisdom and stature, and in favor with you and the people [his/her] life touches. Give [him/her] a listening ear to [his/her] parents' instructions. Help [him/her] to pay attention that [he/she] may gain understanding [Luke 2:52; Prov. 4:1].

May the Spirit of the Lord rest upon my grandchild [name]— the Spirit of wisdom, understanding, counsel, might, knowledge, and the reverential and obedient fear of the Lord. I pray the eyes of [his/her] heart may be enlightened in order that [he/she] may know you better. I pray that Christ may dwell in [name's] heart through faith and that [he/she] will be rooted and established in love [Isa. 11:2; Eph. 1:17; 3:17].[2]

Affirmations

One grandmother affirms aloud what God's Word says about each of her grandchildren as she calls out their names—Joshua, Jeremiah, Jacob, and Abigail. She gives thanks to the Lord that her grandchildren

- are being transformed by the renewing of their minds (Rom. 12:2).
- are saved by grace (Eph. 2:8–9).
- are strengthened with power through his Spirit in the inner man (Eph. 3:13; Heb. 10:19–22).
- are redeemed and forgiven of their trespasses through his blood because of the riches of his grace which he has lavished upon them (Eph. 1:7–8; Col. 1:2).
- are more than conquerors through Christ who loves them (Rom. 8:37).
- have been called by God to a holy calling (2 Tim. 1:9; Heb. 3:1).
- are his workmanship, created for good works (Eph. 2:10).
- are firmly rooted in him (Col. 2:7).
- have been delivered from the domain of darkness and transferred into the kingdom of his beloved Son (Col. 1:13).
- have been given a spirit of power and love and of self-discipline (2 Tim. 1:7).
- have eternal life (John 3:16).
- can do all things through Christ who strengthens them (Phil. 4:13).

Suggested Reading

Bisset, Tom. *Why Christian Kids Leave the Faith*. Grand Rapids: Discovery House, 1997.

Christenson, Evelyn. *What Happens When We Pray for Our Families*. Wheaton: Victor, 1992.

Eastman, Dick, and Jack Hayford. *Living and Praying in Jesus' Name*. Wheaton: Tyndale, 1988.

Endicott, Irene. *Grandparenting: It's Not What It Used to Be*. Nashville: Broadman and Holman, 1997.

Evans, Debra. *Ready or Not, You're a Grandparent*. Colorado Springs: Victor, 1997.

Exley, Helen. *The Love between Grandmothers and Grandchildren*. New York: Hallmark Books, 1997.

Ingram, Kristen Johnson. *I'll Ask My Grandmother—She's Very Wise*. Uhrichville, Ohio: Promise Books, 1999.

Livingstone Corporation. *Personal Promises from God's Word*. Grand Rapids: World, 1996.

Mullins, Traci. *A Grandmother's Touch*. Ann Arbor: Servant, 2001.

Parish, Fawn. *Honor: What Love Looks Like*. Ventura, Calif.: Renew, 1999.

Rikkers, Doris, compiler. *Grandmothers Are a Gift from God*. Grand Rapids: Zondervan, 2000.

Schaeffer, Edith, *What Is a Family?* Grand Rapids: Baker, 1975.

Sheets, Dutch. *The Beginner's Guide to Intercessory Prayer*. Ann Arbor: Servant, 2001.

Sherrer, Quin. *Prayers from a Grandma's Heart*. Grand Rapids: Zondervan, 2002.

Sherrer, Quin, and Ruthanne Garlock. *How to Pray for Your Children*. Ventura, Calif.: Regal, 1998.

_____. *Prayer Partnerships*. Ann Arbor: Servant, 2001.

_____. *Prayers Women Pray*. Ann Arbor: Servant, 1997.

_____. *Praying Prodigals Home*. Ventura, Calif.: Regal, 2000.

Smalley, Gary, and John Trent. *The Blessing*. Nashville: Thomas Nelson, 1986.

Summers, JoAn. *Keepers of the Treasure*. Dallas: Prayer Mountain Press, 2000. (Prayer Mountain Press's address is P.O. Box 210733, Dallas, TX 75211.)

Swope, Mary Ruth. *Bless Your Children Every Day*. Fourth edition. Lone Star, Tex.: Swope Enterprises, 2000.

Notes

Chapter 1: A Grandmother's Spiritual Influence

1. Barbara Johnson, *Leaking Laffs between Pampers and Depends* (Nashville: Word, 2000), 21.

2. Mary Ruth Swope, *Bless Your Children Every Day*, 4th ed. (Lone Star, Tex.: Swope Enterprises, Inc., 2000), 13–16. (Swope Enterprises, Inc., P.O. Box 1290, Lone Star, TX 75668.) Used with permission.

3. Gary Smalley and John Trent, *The Blessing* (Nashville: Thomas Nelson, 1984), 24, 29, 37.

4. Dick Eastman and Jack Hayford, *Living and Praying in Jesus' Name* (Wheaton: Tyndale, 1988), 10. Used with permission. See book for the complete list of names of Christ.

Chapter 2: Praying for Spiritual Growth

1. See Luke 19:10 NKJV; 2 Peter 3:9.

2. "Teens Don't Embrace Truth," *The Church Around the World*, January 2001, 1.

3. See Rom. 10:9–10 and 1 John 1:9; 2:2.

4. Bruce H. Wilkinson, *The Prayer of Jabez* (Sisters, Ore.: Multnomah, 2000), 69.

5. Jay Kesler, *Grandparenting: The Agony and the Ecstasy* (Ann Arbor: Servant, 1993), 99.

Chapter 3: Praying for Homes and Families

1. Karen S. Peterson, "Grandparents Play Key Role, Study Finds," *USA Today*, reprinted in the *San Antonio Express News*, 8 April 2001, p. 1H.

2. From the website http://www.parenting-qa.com.

3. Adapted from Quin Sherrer and Ruthanne Garlock, *How to Pray for Your Children* (Ventura, Calif.: Regal, 1998), 219.

4. Adapted from *Listen, God Is Speaking to You* by Quin Sherrer, © by Quin Sherrer, 107–8. Published by Servant Publications, P.O. Box 8617, Ann Arbor, MI 48107. Used with permission.

5. Quin Sherrer, *Good Night, Lord* (Ventura, Calif.: Regal, 2000), 178–79.

Chapter 5: Praying for Protection and Health

1. Sonja Garza, "Girl's Safe Return Amazes Experts," *San Antonio Express-News*, 11 March 2001, p. 4B.
2. Edith Schaeffer, *What Is a Family?* (Grand Rapids: Baker, 1975), 98, 99.

Chapter 6: Praying for Hurting Grandchildren

1. John Trent, *Quiet Whispers from God's Heart for Parents* (Nashville: J. Countryman, 1999), 99–100.

Chapter 7: Praying for Families Broken by Death or Divorce

1. Irene M. Endicott, *Grandparenting Redefined* (Lynnwood, Wash.: Aglow International, 1991), 73.
2. Jan Stoop and Betty Southard, *The Grandmother Book* (Nashville: Thomas Nelson, 1993), 211–12.
3. Irene Endicott, *Grandparenting: It's Not What It Used to Be* (Nashville: Broadman and Holman, 1997), 161–62.
4. Jay Kesler, *Grandparenting: The Agony and the Ecstasy* (Ann Arbor: Servant, 1993), 182–83.

Chapter 9: Praying for Prodigal Grandchildren

1. Barbara Johnson, *Living Somewhere between Estrogen and Death* (Dallas: Word, 1997), 119.
2. This material is taken from *Why Christian Kids Leave the Faith*, by Tom Bisset, 22–23. Copyright © 1997. Used by permission of Discovery House Publishers, Box 3566, Grand Rapids, Michigan 49501. All rights reserved.
3. Ibid., 205, 206, 207.
4. Paul Billheimer, *Destined for the Throne* (Fort Washington, Pa.: Christian Literature Crusade, 1975), 67–68.
5. Quin Sherrer and Ruthanne Garlock, *Praying Prodigals Home* (Ventura, Calif.: Regal, 2000), 209–10.
6. This material is taken from *Why Christian Kids Leave the Faith*, by Tom Bisset, 157–58. Copyright © 1997. Used by permission of Discovery House Publishers, Box 3566, Grand Rapids, Michigan 49501. All rights reserved.

Chapter 10: Praying for Choices and Turning Points

1. Jack Terry, *The Great Trail Ride* (Eugene, Ore.: Harvest House, 2000), 54.

2. "Music, Family, Sports Help Prevent Drug Use," quoting a 5 December 2000 Associated Press report, *Dateline DREAM*, February/March 2001, p. 4. *Dateline DREAM* is published by Developing Resources for Education in America, Inc., Jackson, Mississippi. The survey cited was part of a "What's Your Anti-Drug?" youth marketing campaign under the auspices of the White House Office of National Drug Control Policy and funded by Congress.

3. Adapted from Quin Sherrer and Ruthanne Garlock, *How to Pray for Your Children* (Ventura, Calif.: Regal, 1998), 206.

Chapter 11: Taking the Role of Parent or Coparent

1. Renate Robey, "Grandparent-Parents Find Help," *Denver Post*, 18 July 1999, 2B.

2. Ibid.

3. Ibid.

4. Adapted from *Listen, God Is Speaking to You*, by Quin Sherrer, © by Quin Sherrer, 66–68. Published by Servant Publications, P.O. Box 8617, Ann Arbor, MI 48107. Used with permission.

Chapter 12: Leaving a Lasting Legacy

1. Dale Evans with Carole C. Carlson, *Our Values* (Grand Rapids: Revell, 1997), 86.

2. Gigi Graham Tchividjian, *Passing It On* (New York: McCracken Press, 1993), 23. Copyright owned by Gigi Graham Tchividjian; used by permission of the author.

3. Ibid., 69.

4. Ibid., 14.

5. Edith Schaeffer, *What Is a Family?* (Grand Rapids: Baker, 1975), 105–7.

Appendix

1. Adapted from Quin Sherrer and Ruthanne Garlock, *How to Pray for Your Children* (Ventura, Calif.: Regal, 1998), 233.

2. Ibid., 46.

Miracles Happen When You Pray

True Stories of the Remarkable Power of Prayer

QUIN SHERRER

If you've ever longed for a miracle . . . if you've ever wondered what could happen if you took God at his Word . . . this book is for you. *Miracles Happen When You Pray* shows that God is still in the miracle-working, life-altering business. He has answered the prayers of many—and he wants to answer your prayers, too. Best-selling author Quin Sherrer offers inspiring stories of ordinary people who prayed and who received extra-ordinary answers. Here are remarkable accounts of healing, protection, direction, and rescue—together with wisdom from the Bible to guide your own prayers. You, too, will be encouraged to pray for miracles—and your faith will be strengthened as you discover the reality of the depth of God's love for you, his child.

Softcover   0-310-20997-8

Pick up a copy today at your favorite bookstore!

ZONDERVAN™

GRAND RAPIDS, MICHIGAN 49530

www.zondervan.com